AF574318

EMERGENCY AND HIGH SPEED DRIVING TECHNIQUES

EMERGENCY AND HIGH SPEED DRIVING TECHNIQUES

JOHN M. CLARK, JR.

Gulf Publishing Company, Book Division, Houston, Texas

Emergency and High Speed Driving Techniques

Library of Congress
Catalog Card Number:
76-1675

ISBN: 0-87201-256-5

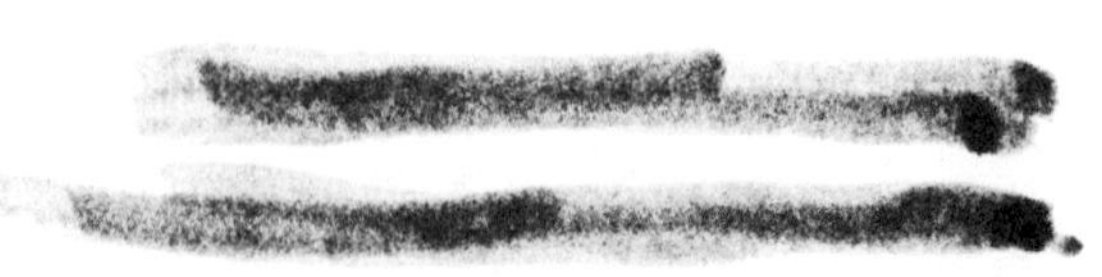

This book is dedicated
to Betty Jean.
Without her gentle
but persistent urgings
it probably would
never have been written.

CONTENTS

Preface ix

1 It's More Than Speed 1

2 Vehicle Control 9

3 Braking 38

4 Tire Design 55

5 Expect the Unexpected 79

6 You, The Driver 92

7 Restraint Systems 105

8 High Speed Pursuit 115

9 Maintenance 122

Index 127

PREFACE

The purpose of this emergency driving book is to fill the void that has existed in the technical literature of emergency vehicle operation.

I became aware of the need for this type of book after conducting a series of Emergency Medical Service (EMS) driver training courses for the city of San Antonio. Like several San Antonio physicians and surgeons, my services were contributed as a public service to help make the EMS "go." And "go" it has! San Antonians are intensely proud, and justifiably so, of the EMS technicians who are providing the city and all of Bexar County with a life-saving ambulance service. As one newspaper reporter has written, "The EMS technicians have attained the status of 'folk heroes' in the eyes of San Antonio citizens."

In eighteen months the EMS drivers of San Antonio amassed a total of more than 700,000 miles without a single injury. I feel that the week of classroom and on-the-course driving instruction given to all San Antonio EMS drivers contributed to this safety record.

This book has been written to combine in a single publication the years of experience in driving vehicles at the "limits of adhesion" with published and unpublished engineering data as to what initiates loss of control in a high speed evasive driving maneuver. Although written with the police and other emergency vehicle drivers in mind, the information in this book is applicable to the operation of any vehicle driven above normal speeds. In fact, the information will be of considerable value to the average driver because even the average driver experiences conditions where he has marginal or no control over his vehicle. By understanding what causes loss of vehicle control the average driver is better prepared to avoid a dangerous vehicle handling situation. My interest in the stability and handling of vehicles in emergency driving maneuvers started in the late '50s when I was comparing the handling of competitive makes of vehicles of like size, weight, and purchase price. Being a research automotive engineer, I was fascinated by these studies, so I joined the sports car racing movement through the Sports Car Club of America to further study vehicle response in maximum effort handling maneuvers. After qualifying for a National Competition driving license and actively competing for several years, I served as a certified racing driver instructor. In conducting classroom instruction for aspiring racing drivers I became aware of how little even skilled drivers actually know about the causes and effects of vehicle control.

Over the past sixteen years I have been engaged in field testing of vehicles, high speed braking and cornering studies, intensive studies of causes for individual highway accidents, and various highway safety programs. I have not included any material in this manual that has not been "proven out" on the race track or vehicle test course. Other data has been derived from carefully conducted engineering tests or experiments.

I wish to thank Officer Joseph Stolowski, a top level pursuit driver of the San Antonio Police Department, for his aid in the preparation of the chapter on "Pursuit Driving." Not all of his excellent suggestions were included since this is not a "how-to-do-it" police manual, but a book on emergency driving techniques.

I am also indebted to Capt. Ed "Moose" Sebera, a dedicated officer of the San Antonio EMS, for his helpful suggestions in the preparation of the ambulance related portions of the book.

Many thanks are due Ms. J.T. Shwiff for her invaluable aid in typing and editing and to Mr. Jesse Medina for his preparation of the graphs and illustrations.

The student emergency vehicle driver should carefully study the material gathered together in this book. Understanding the points covered in this book might save a life—yours! Remember you are "playing for keeps" in this game and there is no room for error.

John M. Clark, Jr.
February, 1976

EMERGENCY AND HIGH SPEED DRIVING TECHNIQUES

Besides quick reflexes, you need sound judgement.

1 IT'S MORE THAN SPEED

This book presents in readable form for non-technical persons the important "do's and don'ts" of emergency driving. The material has been gathered from years of experience in high speed vehicle testing and race driving, as well as from engineering sources.

No one is a "born emergency driver." Some people think they are and their ignorance leads them into serious trouble, including fatal accidents.

There are two ways to learn emergency driving. One is through experience, which can be lengthy, dangerous, and very expensive. Another, more desirable way is to learn the important lessons in the classroom and then support this with "on-the-course" training, which should include handling a vehicle at the "limit of adhesion" in various simulated road conditions. "Limit of adhesion" means that the vehicle is being driven through a maneuver at the highest possible speed without losing control. As we will see later, this can be at a very precise speed for any given curve.

There are basically only two things that can be done in safely controlling an emergency vehicle; (1) change speed by braking or accelerating and (2) change the direction by steering. This, of course, is an oversimplification of emergency driving, just as it is an oversimplification to say that all one does in tennis is bat the ball across the net before it bounces twice. There is much to learn in the classroom, on the test course, and hopefully to a lesser extent, by actual, "on-the-job" mistakes. Because this book cannot describe every road condition or potential accident situation, there must be some learning by field experience. However, the main intention of this book is to provide the students of emergency driving with those driving skills and techniques needed to safely and efficiently operate their vehicles under any emergency condition.

There is a special aptitude for high speed emergency driving. Just as some people can maintain a bowling average of 250, or carry a golf handicap of two, some people are more adept at being emergency drivers than others. If on-the-course training has been planned, it is sincerely hoped that you will pass the driving course and be recommended unconditionally as an emergency vehicle driver. However, because the instructor has a deep responsibility to the driving public, to you, and to your team members, you should realize that the instructor cannot recommend you as a driver if he feels you would be unsafe to yourself and to others.

Part of that special aptitude and something that cannot be described in this book is the ability to anticipate thorugh your "seat-of-the-pants" the approaching loss of adhesion by the tires. Only by experiencing the approaching loss of adhesion and subsequent loss of control on the driving course can one understand the feeling. It is far better to face this "moment of truth" on a wide open airport ramp or cleared super market parking lot than on a crowded public street. It is also far easier and cheaper on vehicles and drivers!

If you are to be an emergency driver and it is time for you to take your turn behind the wheel of the vehicle on a public highway you assume an awesome responsibility. You have the responsibility to the driving public, and you should feel a very deep sense of responsibility to the other member or members of your team. The entire idea behind any emergency vehicle operation is the saving of lives, not the destruction of lives and property through careless driving. As an EMS or ambulance driver you have an added responsibility: the patient on the litter.

When you have a life in balance on the litter and every second counts in getting to the hospital, then a Code 3 run may be justified. But, every run need not be made in this manner as many private ambulance drivers tend to do. It must be kept foremost in your mind that the life that you are attempting to preserve can be further jeopardized by either a panic braking stop, loss of control, abrupt swerving, or impact with another vehicle. Any of these actions can cause the death of the patient and the injury or death of another driver, a bicycle rider, or a pedestrian.

At each intersection, at each traffic congested area, it will be necessary for you to calculate your risk in getting through safely with speed or slowing down and ensuring that you get through the intersection or congested traffic area without incident.

Closed Loop Systems

High speed emergency driving involves two closed loop systems.

The first closed loop system is the driver-vehicle closed loop of Figure 1.1. This system basically concerns the "rapport" between the driver and his vehicle. It involves the following steps: the driver applies corrective steering or braking, the vehicle responds, the driver feels the vehicle respond, and corrects the steering or braking maneuver. All of this turns around and around in the closed loop system with continuous input by the driver to the vehicle, and feedback from the vehicle telling the driver *what the vehicle needs* to keep it safely under control. This is particularly true when driving through cor-

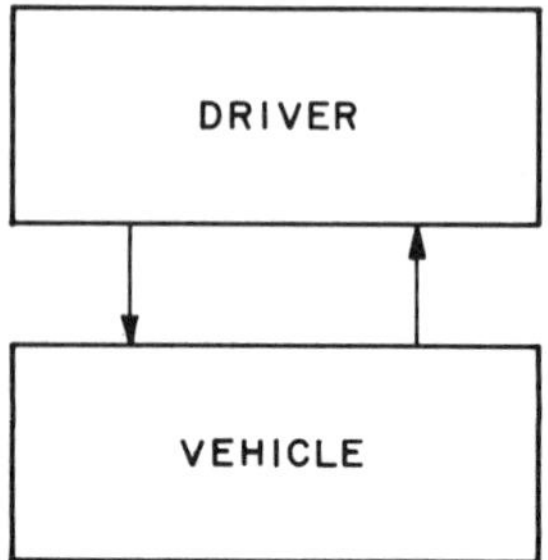

Figure 1.1. The driver-vehicle closed loop system involves a series of driver actions and vehicle responses.

ners near the limits of adhesion, braking on icy roads, driving on rainslick or snow covered highways at higher than normal speeds, and other maneuvers that require constant and rapid driver-to-vehicle closed loop feedback.

The other loop, shown in Figure 1.2, is the environment-driver-vehicle closed loop system in which the environment presents a problem in the road ahead to the driver of the vehicle. The driver evaluates the situation in his own mental computer, decides on the input that should be fed back to the vehicle, and then steers, brakes, or accelerates, as the case may be, to avoid the problem. The vehicle's movement establishes a new relationship between the vehicle and the environment. The driver evaluates this new relationship and starts back through the closed loop system again. Although this process is a series of separate actions, a good driver must be able to repeat these actions quickly and smoothly, making them appear as one concerted effort.

Mastery of this closed loop system by the driver determines the difference between an irresponsible driver and a very careful one. An experienced, cautious driver evaluates the situation ahead and anticipates the movement and the probable position of other vehicles by the time his own vehicle reaches that spot. Too often careless drivers dash into expressway traffic, brake quickly to avoid hitting the cars they have overtaken, and force the vehicles around them to take evasive action. Such driving tactics indicate a definite break in their environment-driver-vehicle closed loop system because their mental computer has not received feedback telling them that emergency action will be required if they continue at their approach speed.

Too many drivers regard driving as merely a sometime thing, something that requires occasional attention while they converse with the person in the seat beside them, gaze at the passing scenery, or otherwise divert their attention from the road ahead. A careful driver, and this is the only way an emergency vehicle driver should operate his vehicle, *maintains vigilance 100% of the time.* The experienced emergency driver is constantly taking the feedback from the environment and evaluating the situation, evaluating the changing traffic pattern ahead of him, and attempting to predict whether that person coming down off the entrance ramp is going to charge out into traffic, or whether he is going to wait for the traffic to move on through without starting panic braking on the expressway.

Obviously, mastery of the environment-driver-vehicle closed loop system is something that we cannot learn out of a book. It is something that we have to learn through experience, through perception, and through evaluation of some

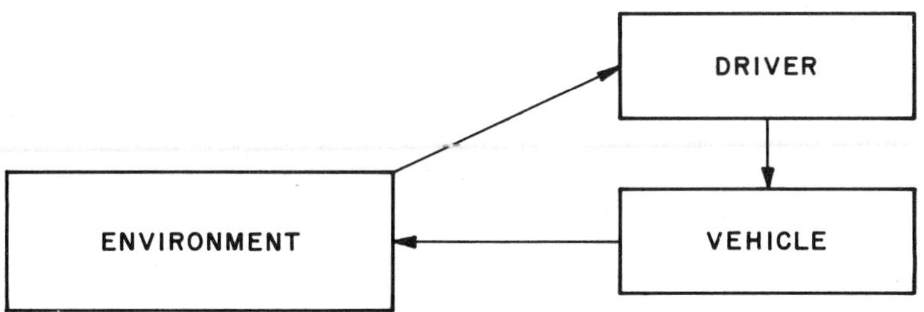

Figure 1.2. In the environment-driver-vehicle closed system the driver must react to environmental conditions as well as vehicle conditions.

of the clues that we can obtain from observing the movement of the vehicles ahead. If the vehicle coming down the exit ramp is a "muscle car" with rally stripes, wide tires, and possibly a smashed-in fender or door, it is a good bet that this isn't a careful driver. This is probably a driver who has "smoked his tires" before and may do it again, right in front of you. If the vehicle is a big semi-trailer or flat-bed loaded with brick or a load of heavy steel and the vehicle is coming down the entrance ramp rapidly, then it is safe to assume that; (a) the vehicle is not going to be able to brake, (b) it is going to come out into the traffic lane, and (c) the traffic is going to have to open up for the vehicle. If this is occurring, obviously a dangerous traffic situation is developing ahead of you, so it is time to start increasing the distance between you and that situation by getting your foot on the brake, and starting to slow your vehicle down.

The dangerous environment is not limited to the road ahead. Many times you will be driving a vehicle at moderate speeds and you will be overtaken by speeders who are weaving through expressway traffic, changing lanes, and endangering vehicles on all sides. This particular driver may be the reason for one of your next emergency runs! In the meantime, however, you have to evaluate his movements with respect to the traffic ahead and determine your best course of action to avoid being swept into a serious traffic situation by his wild maneuvers.

The top level emergency vehicle driver has developed by experience and instinct a special ability to anticipate the next movement of his vehicle and to begin a controlling maneuver before it actually is required. After the break-away or loss of control of a vehicle is initiated, it is often too late to recover. Then we can only salvage what we can and make the best recovery possible! The top level driver has anticipated the break-away before it occurs. This is what is called being "in rhythm" with your vehicle. A good driver seems to be an integral part of the machine. High speed emergency driving requires a smooth flow of steering, braking, and accelerating that alters the attitude and the speed of the vehicle to correct an impending loss of control. In contrast, the poor driver is rough, "out of rhythm" with his vehicle. He feeds in a correction and observes what happens, feeds in another correction, and waits to observe what happens. This mechanical step-by-step driving style is the mark of the inexperienced driver or an experienced driver who will never gain true proficiency in handling his vehicle. An experienced driving instructor need only ride a block with a person in order to evaluate driving proficiency from the driver-vehicle feedback loop system which tells the instructor that this person in "in rhythm" with his vehicle or that he is badly "out of rhythm." Then, of course, there is the driver who is proficient in handling his vehicle, but who was not born with a good mental computer system which permits him to evaluate the approaching environment. We see this in many teenage drivers who do an excellent job of handling the vehicle, but charge in "where angels fear to tread." So, the driver has to be master of both closed-loop systems to be truly a careful and proficient driver.

It is essential that you be reminded constantly of the importance of every-second-attention to the driving task in front of you. Later you will be shown what a one-second delay means in applying the brakes in an emergency situation. One second of inattention can mean the difference between a serious, possibly fatal, accident and stopping in time.

As mentioned previously, there are only two things that you can do to control your vehicle; change its direction and change its speed. To accomplish either of these, it is necessary to maintain continuous *rolling contact* between the tires and the road surface. *Rolling contact* is the key because once the tires are "locked up" and rapid sliding on the road surface begins, the vehicle has passed the limit of adhesion, and is out of control.

This rolling contact between the bottom surfaces of the tires and the road surface is called the footprint area of the tires

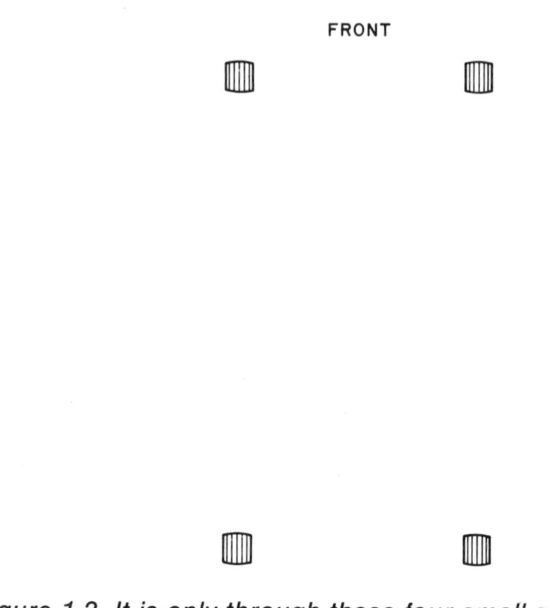

Figure 1.3. It is only through these four small spots that all the steering and braking of a vehicle is transmitted.

(see Figure 1.3). These footprints are each about the width of a tread and 8-10″ long on the typical modular ambulance and 7½″ long on a typical police vehicle. It is *only* through the action of the tires on these four small spots that we start, stop, and steer the vehicle. Your life, your passengers' lives, and the lives of those who are affected by the movement of your vehicle are dependent upon your ability to maintain a smooth rolling contact of the footprints with the surface of the road. Therefore, it is extremely important that you learn what makes a tire *develop* traction and, even more important, what makes it *lose* traction.

Staying on the road is
what it's all about.

2 VEHICLE CONTROL

Tire characteristics and vehicle control are closely related because vehicle control is completely dependent upon the tire footprints maintaining constant *rolling contact* with the road surface. Understanding how a tire performs under limit-of-adhesion conditions is very important because such knowledge can help you avoid maneuvers that will cause your tires to lose their grip on the road, "the stiction" that controls your vehicle.

How a Tire Steers

It may surprise you to learn that a tire rarely rolls around a corner like the flanged wheel of a railroad car riding an iron rail. Only at very low speeds (1 to 2 mph) does the tire roll around in this simple guided manner. However, as speed increases, tire performance changes. In Figure 2.1 we are looking up at the tire as it rolls along over a glass plate. Figure 2.1A shows the tire rolling straight ahead, parallel to the vehicle's direction of travel. As a result, there is no side force and the vehicle continues in a straight line. The glass surface

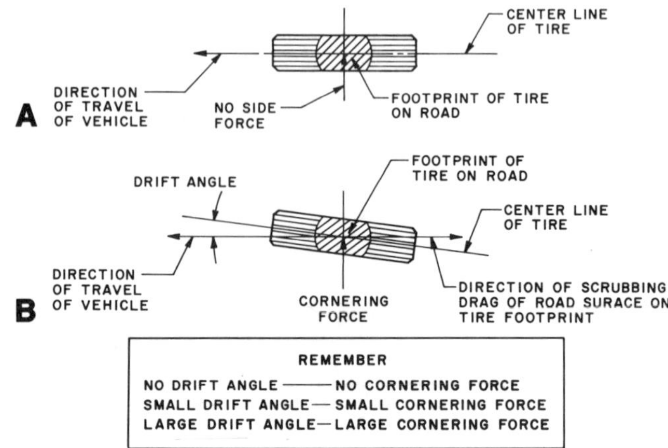

Figure 2.1. Drawing A *shows how a tire traveling in a straight line has no side force or cornering force acting upon it. Drawing* B *shows the cornering force and scrubbing drag which are generated when a tire is steered.*

under each tire is supporting approximately one-fourth of the vehicle's weight.

In Figure 2.1B the tire is being steered and a small drift angle is being introduced to the tire. *Drift angle* is that angle formed between the centerline of the tire and the line indicating the vehicle's instantaneous direction of travel. As the drift angle increases, so does the scrubbing drag of the tire across the surface of the roadway. This scrubbing action creates a cornering force, which, in trying to shove the tire over changes the vehicle's direction.

We know instinctively that as more steering is applied to a vehicle, more cornering force is developed and the vehicle tends to go around a turn in a smaller radius of curvature. In other words, more steering increases the drift angle or the direction of the centerline of the front tires relative to the vehicle's instantaneous direction. At zero drift angle there is no cornering force. A *small drift angle,* causes a *small cornering force* and a *large drift angle* causes a *large cornering force.*

The start of a drift angle, the introduction of a steering angle to the front tires, does not necessarily set up an immediate cornering force. You can check this on an open highway with no traffic by quickly flipping the steering wheel 10-20° and then quickly returning the steering wheel back to its former position. There is little change in the attitude or direction of the vehicle. This inherent steering lag causes a tire to move straight ahead for a short distance before developing the side force or cornering force which causes the tire and vehicle to move toward the direction in which it is steered. This is shown clearly in Figure 2.2. However, the time required for

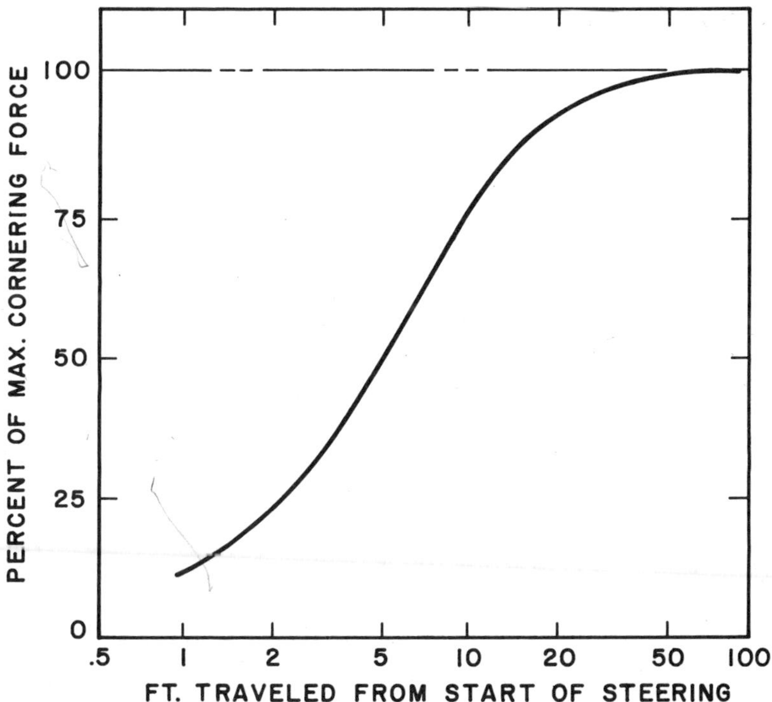

Figure 2.2. This graph shows the distance traveled in developing full cornering force on a steered tire. (Used with permission of the Society of Automotive Engineers, Inc., Warrendale, Pa.)

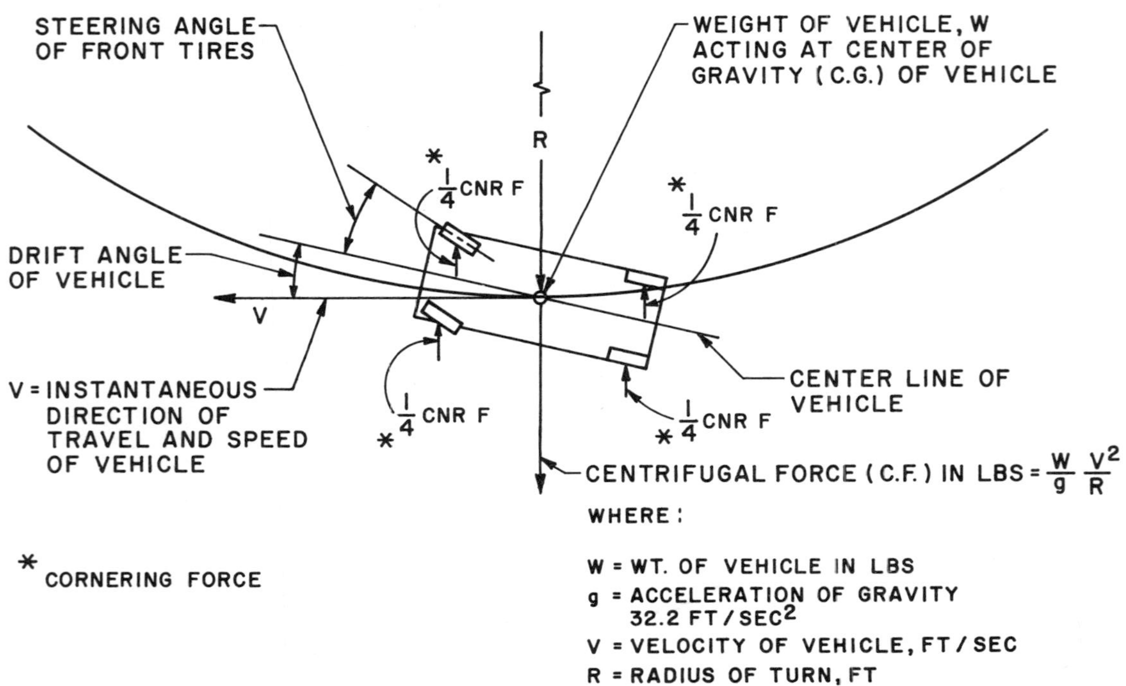

Figure 2.3. These are the forces acting on a cornering vehicle in a constant radius turn.

the tire to develop full cornering force varies with the road surface and other factors. Steel belted radial tires in particular, have a very low lag, with almost immediate response, to steering correction.

The Forces Affecting Vehicle Control

Before we deal with what happens to the rear tires in a turn, let's look at the action of the entire vehicle in a constant radius turn. Figure 2.3 shows a vehicle in a constant radius turn. The vehicle's center of gravity is moving about the center of the turn at the constant radius *R*. Any weight moving about a center at a constant radius will have a centrifugal force acting upon it, that is, a force that is trying to keep the weight traveling in a straight line rather than allowing it to keep going around in a circle. Figure 2.4 gives a simple interpretation of how we all as children have experienced centrifugal force and found that it was a very real force which increased sharply as we swung the weight faster and faster in its circular path. Actually, centrifugal force is equal to the velocity squared divided by the radius of the turn times the acceleration of gravity. Since the centrifugal force increases as the square of the speed, doubling the speed increases the centrifugal force four times. Mathematically, the centrifugal force, in units of gravity, is equal to

$$C.F. = V^2/gR \qquad (2.1)$$

where

V = Velocity, (ft/sec)
g = Acceleration of gravity, (32.2 ft/sec^2)
R = Radius of circular path, (ft)

To obtain the actual pull in pounds of centrifugal force we multiply the answer from Equation (2.1) by the weight of the

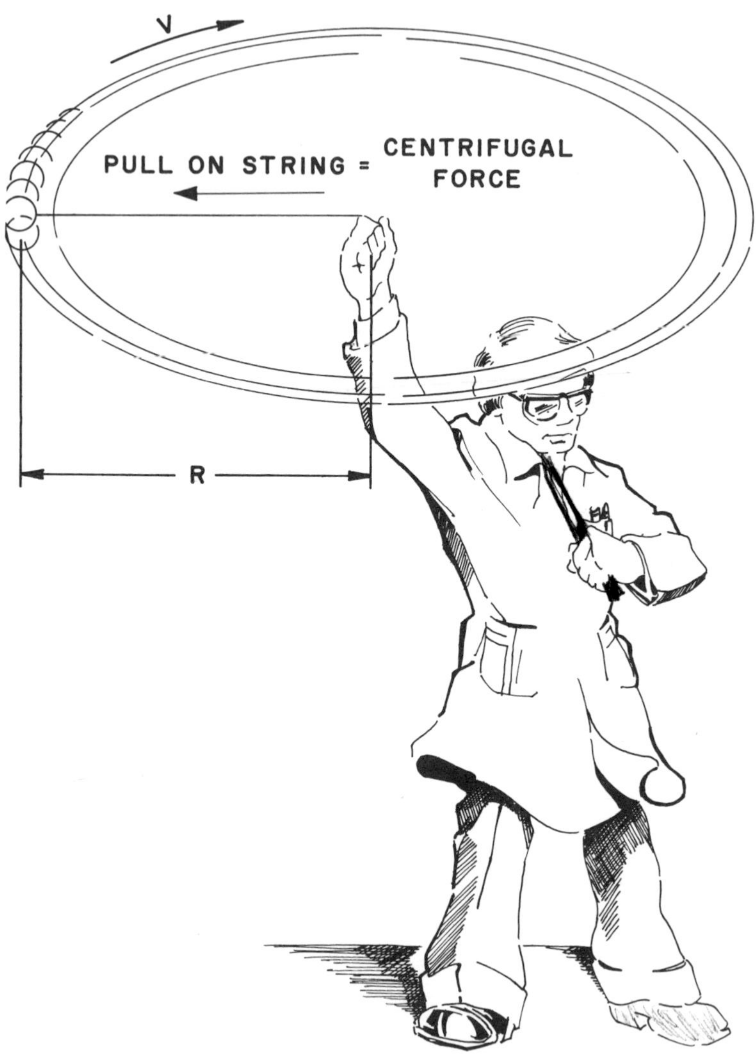

Figure 2.4. This is a simple interpretation of how centrifugal force acts upon a string attached to an object moving in a circle.

object. That is, if we are cornering fast enough to develop 0.5g and the weight of our vehicle is 4000 lbs:

$$(0.5)\ 4000 = 2000 \text{ lbs of centrifugal force}$$

To provide the total cornering force needed to keep the vehicle in a constant radius turn, the front and rear tires must each supply part of the force. The sum of cornering force on the front tires plus the cornering force on the rear tires must equal the total centrifugal force acting on the vehicle; the entire 2000 lbs in the previous example. If the cornering force should be removed on all four tires the vehicle would continue along the straight line represented by the vector V (Figure 2.3), which is the instantaneous direction of travel of the vehicle. This is what happens on an icy road when the tires skid and lose all cornering force. The vehicle simply goes off the corner in a straight line. We shall see later that the same thing can happen under panic braking in a turn where all cornering force disappears. The vehicle simply leaves the corner in a straight line.

As shown in Figure 2.3 we cannot steer the rear tires and thus develop a drift angle. Yet, if the vehicle is to stay in the turn, the rear tires must develop the remaining cornering force not supplied by the front tires. The vehicle does this for us automatically by developing a *vehicle drift angle,* which is the angle the *vehicle* makes with its instantaneous direction. For the rear tires, vehicle drift angle is the tire drift angle. For the front tires the tire drift angle is the vehicle drift angle *plus* or *minus* the steering angle of the front wheels. Remember, no drift angle—no side force or cornering force, small drift angle—small cornering force, large drift angle—large cornering force. The centrifugal force merely forces the back end of the vehicle out in a drift angle until the rear tires develop enough cornering force to balance their share of the centrifugal force acting on the entire vehicle. To illustrate this a

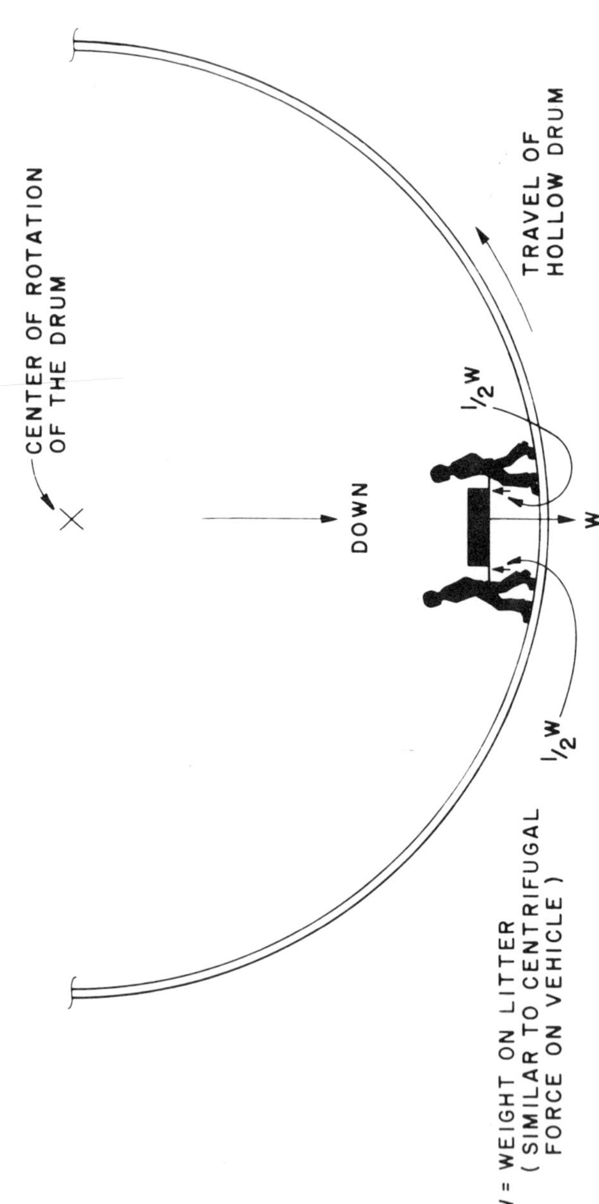

Figure 2.5. This drawing, showing two men carrying a stretcher in a rotating drum, demonstrates how centrifugal force acts upon a cornering vehicle.

little clearer, let's look at Figure 2.5. Imagine two men carrying a litter with weight *W* walking around the inside of a hollow drum. The drum is turning at a specific speed so that the men are always at the bottom of the drum. If the weight *W* is evenly distributed on the litter, then each one of them must supply ½ *W* pounds to hold up his end of the litter. Now imagine that the front man represents the front tires and the rear man represents the rear tires of the cornering vehicle. If the center of gravity of the vehicle is in the center of the vehicle (as we shall see later, this is not always the case), then the front tires must supply half of the centrifugal force and the rear tires must supply the other half to keep the system in balance. Centrifugal force is similar to the force of gravity but it can act in any direction, unlike gravity which only acts downward. In a cornering vehicle centrifugal force is acting parallel to the surface of the ground.

We have discussed to some extent the tire drift angle and its resultant side force that can be resolved into a cornering force and a drag force as shown in Figure 2.6. Note that under cornering the footprint is distorted because of roll-under or distortion of the tire tread by the side force. Note the pneumatic trail in Figure 2.6, which shows that the center of action of the side force does not act exactly through the tire's axis. This results from inertia acting on the tread causing the side force to move rearward. This inertia is caused by the tire tread being "snatched up" off the ground by the hoop strength of the tire. Actually, this is beneficial in that it provides a self-aligning torque that tends to straighten the tire out along the direction of motion. We can feel this in steering through a heavy corner when the self-aligning tire attempts to straighten the steering wheel in our hands.

Let's consider the drag force now. The side force generated by the tire sliding along in a drift angle acts perpendicular to the plane of the tire. However, the cornering force, which holds the vehicle in the turn, acts perpendicular to the vehicle's instantaneous direction. The side force is actually the vector

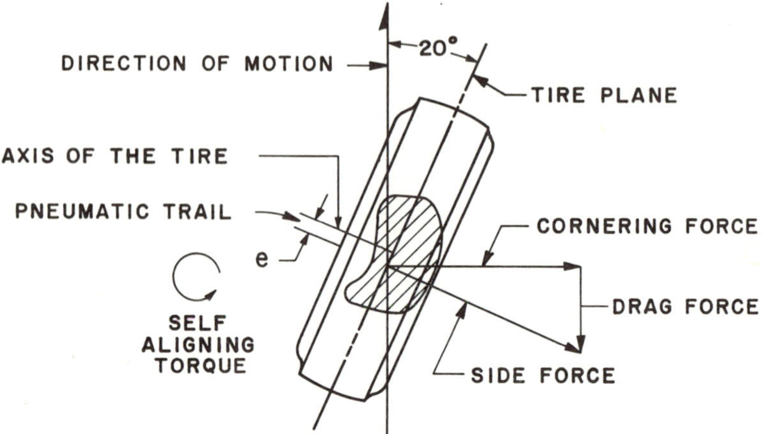

Figure 2.6. Shown here are the self-aligning torque, pneumatic trail, and the cornering, drag, and side forces acting on a tire with a 20° drift angle.

sum of the cornering force plus the drag force, that is, it is the hypotenuse of the triangle (see Figure 2.6). The cornering force and drag force are generated automatically as the vehicle goes into a drift angle. This drag force acts as a very effective braking force to slow down the speed of the vehicle as it goes through a corner. At an approximate maximum drift angle of 20°, the drag force is equal to 36% of the total cornering force which, in plain terms, means that on dry pavement with this high drift angle, there is as much stopping power being generated by the drag force alone, as there is generated in a maximum braking effort on wet pavement. This can be a very important point when you have entered into a curve slightly above the maximum allowable entering speed for maintaining control. It is possible, without touching the brakes, to "scrub off" the excess speed and to quickly slow the vehicle to a speed which allows safe maneuvering through the corner.

There are many points that must be made clear to the emergency driver relative to tire performance and how it affects vehicle handling. Each point will be explained one at a time, and reviewed to determine its interacting effect.

Figure 2.7 describes one of the most important performance characteristics. On dry pavement the cornering coefficient or cornering force steadily increases with the drift angle, until the drift angle reaches about 10° where the cornering coefficient levels off. On wet pavement the cornering force is considerably lower and the coefficient levels off at about 13-14°. The shape of the wet curve depends mainly on the pavement surface, but Figure 2.7 shows typical performance for the average tire. Going back to the dry performance, when the tire is drifted at a higher angle than 18-20° the tire starts to *lose* cornering force. Depending upon the construction of the tire, the loss of cornering force at higher drift angles can be very sharp. A vehicle that is cornering with a vehicle drift angle of approximately 17-18° would be described as taking a corner at the upper

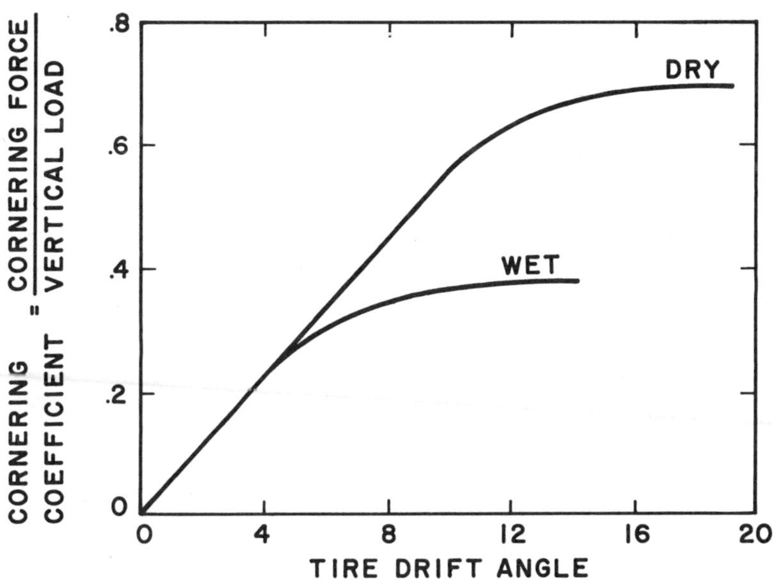

Figure 2.7. This is a graph of the typical cornering coefficient plotted against tire drift angle. (Used with permission of the Society of Automotive Engineers, Inc., Warrendale, Pa.)

limit of adhesion. The tires would be developing a maximum cornering force to hold it in the corner and a higher speed would merely force the vehicle out of the turn since there would be no reserve cornering force left to meet the increased centrifugal force requirement.

It should be stressed that Figure 2.7 shows the cornering coefficient or available cornering force versus tire drift angle for a *free rolling tire* with *no braking* or *traction* applied to the tire. As we apply either braking or traction, the available cornering force is reduced for any given drift angle. However, the higher the drift angle is, the more critical the braking effect will be because the tire is already almost developing its maximum adhesion potential in cornering force. The footprint can only develop a maximum of "x" lbs of adhesion in any direction. The vector sum of the braking plus cornering force must very nearly equal, at all times, the "x" lbs of adhesion. Thus, if braking force is increased, the cornering force must decrease so the sum of the two does not exceed "x" lbs of adhesion. This is why it will be stressed that upon entering into a curve at the limit of adhesion we release the brakes or take our foot off the accelerator. The driver establishes the correct vehicle drift angle, and then, after having stabilized the vehicle in the turn, it is possible for the driver to start smoothly applying power again if the drag force has appreciably slowed the vehicle below the maximum safe cornering speed through the curve. The cornering maneuver will be discussed later in more detail.

Figure 2.8 is a simplified chart showing the extent to which braking can reduce the cornering coefficient or cornering force for a given drift angle. As an illustration, presume that a vehicle is cornering with a drift angle of 16° and a driver applies 25% of maximum braking effort. By increasing the vehicle drift angle up to the maximum of 19-20°, the driver is still unable to regain the loss in cornering force. There is a loss of control and the vehicle leaves the road surface. At increased levels of braking effort, the effective cornering force is further reduced and with complete lockup or panic braking, the cor-

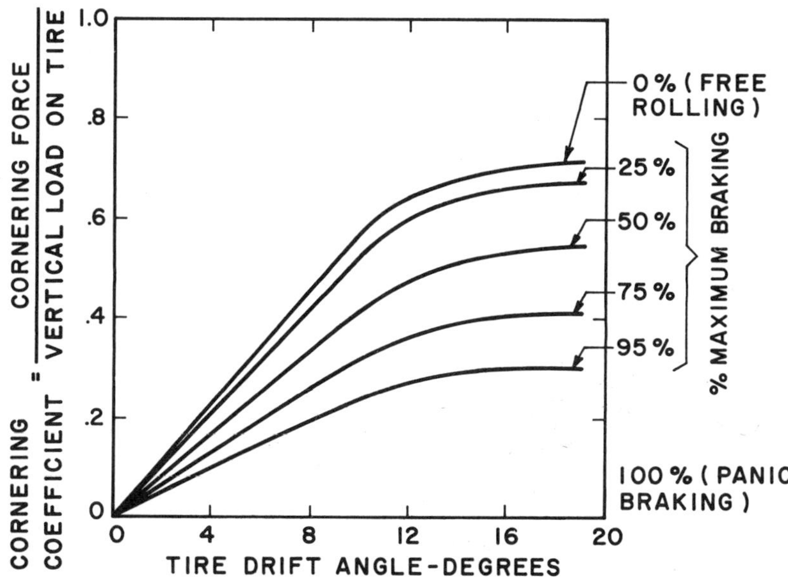

Figure 2.8. These curves for cornering coefficient vs tire drift angle and percent of maximum braking demonstrate how braking can reduce cornering force for a given drift angle.

nering force completely disappears and the vehicle will leave the curve in a straight line. When the vehicle is in a high drift angle of 18-19°, the drag force acting on each tire will be equal to 35-40% of maximum braking effort *while still retaining full cornering force on the tires.* It is extremely difficult to convince the student emergency driver that the worse possible thing to do when he has entered a corner at the limit of adhesion is to apply brakes or use the accelerator.

Driving traction, because of the thrust on the rear wheels, causes loss of cornering force just as braking does. A majority of the student emergency drivers will try to "dirt track" their vehicles through a corner at the limit of adhesion resulting in a rear end breakaway. If, the driver releases the accelerator after feeling the rear wheels "breaking loose" in a loss-of-

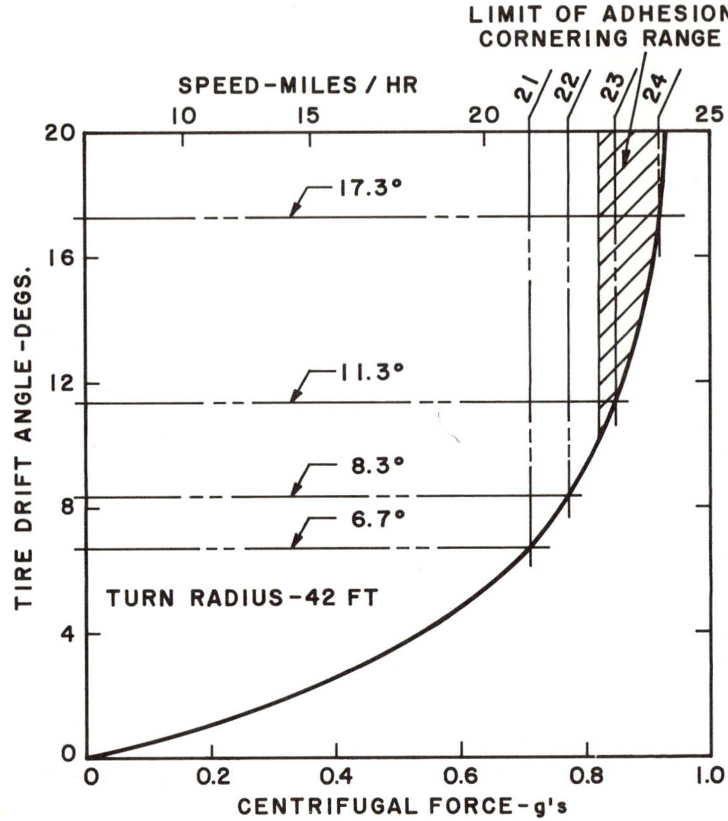

Figure 2.9. Tire drift angle vs centrifugal force and speed for a 47-ft turn radius.

control maneuver, the vehicle quickly regains cornering force on the rear tires while the vehicle is in a high drift angle. A real danger arises here because if the drift angle is high enough, the sudden increase in cornering force can cause the high center of gravity modular ambulances to lift the inside wheels off the ground.

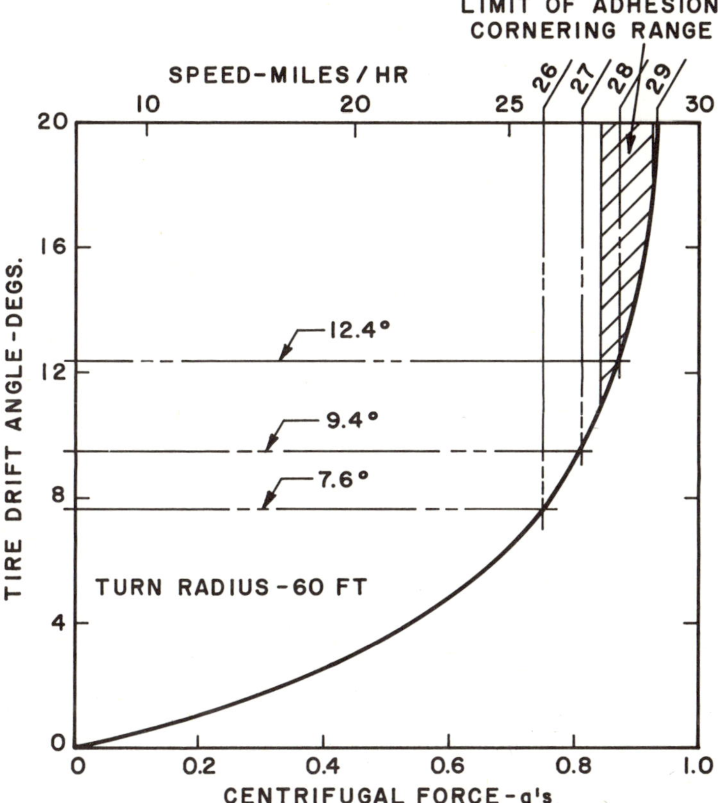

Figure 2.10. Tire drift angle vs centrifugal force and speed for a 60-ft turn radius.

"Cornering Techniques"

Each vehicle has a definite top speed for entering into a curve of given radius. This is illustrated clearly in Figures 2.9 through 2.13 where tire drift angle is plotted vs. centrifugal force and miles per hour. In these curves the "limit-of-

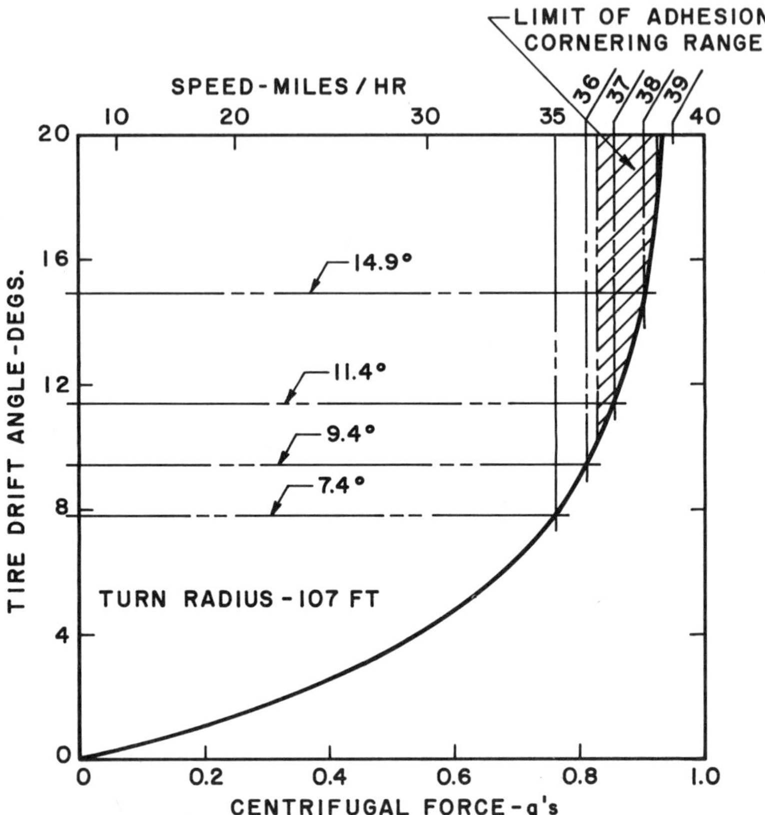

Figure 2.11. Tire drift angle vs centrifugal force and speed for a 107-ft turn radius.

adhesion cornering range" is defined as the centrifugal force range where a minimum tire drift angle of 10° and a maximum of 18° is required. Referring to Figure 2.9, despite the fact that the tire drift angle almost doubles in this range the actual centrifugal force increase is small (13%) and the speed range is narrow (1 to 3 mph) because of the greatly reduced cornering force per degree of tire drift angles above 10°. This tire characteristic makes the critical or maximum allowable

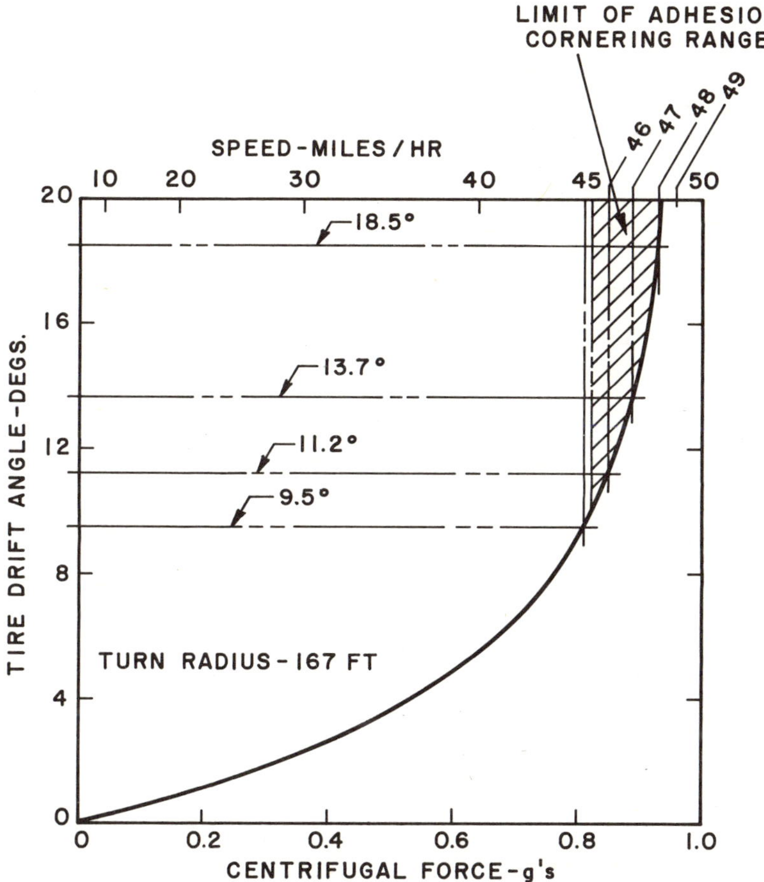

Figure 2.12. Tire drift angle vs centrifugal force and speed for a 167-ft turn radius.

entering speed into a curve extremely important. In the 42-ft radius corner shown in Figure 2.9 the difference between easy, safe control through the corner at 22 mph and start of "breakaway" at 24 mph is only 2 miles per hour! Reviewing Figures 2.10 through 2.13 it can be seen that the "limit-of-adhesion cornering range" and the maximum speed for enter-

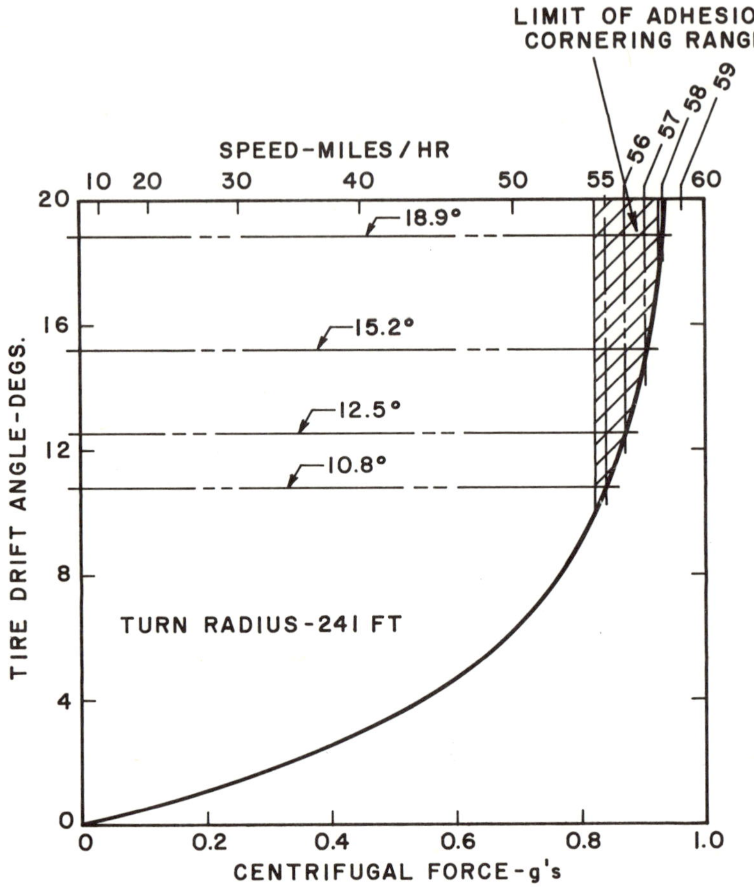

Figure 2.13. Tire drift angle vs cornering force and speed for a 241-ft turn radius.

ing into a curve increase as the radius of the turn increases. Figure 2.14 illustrates this trend clearly with almost a linear increase of maximum cornering speed as the radius is increased. Study these graphs carefully since it is important to fully appreciate how important it is to avoid entering a curve at excessive speed. *Excessive* may mean only 2-3 miles per hour above a comfortable cornering speed through a particular curve.

Experienced emergency drivers in test driving vehicles through a fixed radius curve find that the "breakaway" speed (loss of control) can be repeated with different skilled test drivers driving the same test vehicle. In road racing all vehicles of a given type will be seen going through a corner at the same rate of speed. *After* the corner the vehicles will change positions but in going through the corner all vehicles remain at the same speed, the *maximum possible* cornering speed. To drive through the corner faster would mean loss of control and a "spin out." The narrow allowable margin of error in "limit-of-adhesion cornering," as shown in Figure 2.9 through 2.14, points out the danger of "pushing your vehicle to the limit through a corner."

Figure 2.15 illustrates how critical the correct speed through the turn actually is for a typical suburban street intersection. For 24-ft wide streets a 55-ft radius turn is the maximum practical radius that can be driven with reasonable curb clearance on all sides. The maximum limit-of-adhesion speed for dry roads at a centrifugal force level of 0.9*g* is 27½ mph. This develops an 18° drift angle on the tires and the vehicle is at the "ragged edge" of breakaway. By slowing down only 3½ mph to an entry speed of 24 mph the centrifugal force drops to 0.7*g* and the tire drift angle is reduced to a relatively low 6½°. Yet, it only requires 0.31 second more to go through the turn at 24 mph. Why risk the other persons' lives and your own for less than a third of a second?

Note that the turn must be started at 38 ft (over 1½ widths of the street) from the corner. This means the tires must *start developing full cornering force* 38 ft from the corner. At 24 mph the vehicle is traveling 35 ft/sec. If we allow ¼ second to develop full cornering:

$$\tfrac{1}{4}\,(35) = 8.75 \text{ ft}$$
$$38 + 8.75 = 46.75 \text{ ft}$$

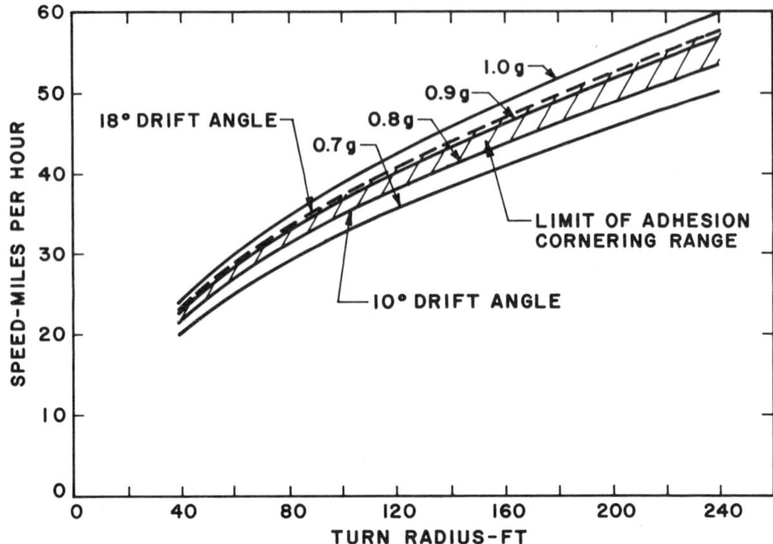

Figure 2.14. This graph illustrates the speed range for limit-of-adhesion cornering for various turn radii.

So, the turn must be *started* almost 47 ft from the corner. This is an important point to remember when practicing on-the-course driver training. Start your corner soon enough! If you do, you will find the vehicle moves easily into "the groove" (the correct turn path) and negotiating the corner is easy and smooth. Drivers who have not received emergency driving instruction invariably go "too deep" into the turn before starting to corner their vehicle. As a result they have to make a hard quick turn to keep from hitting the curb on the intersection street (Point A on Figure 2.15). If you start your turn too soon it is easier (and far smoother) to increase your turn radius to avoid the curb on the inside of your turn than it is to shorten your turn radius when you have gone "too deep" into the corner before starting to turn. Practice starting your turn soon enough and you'll be surprised how it smooths out your cornering technique.

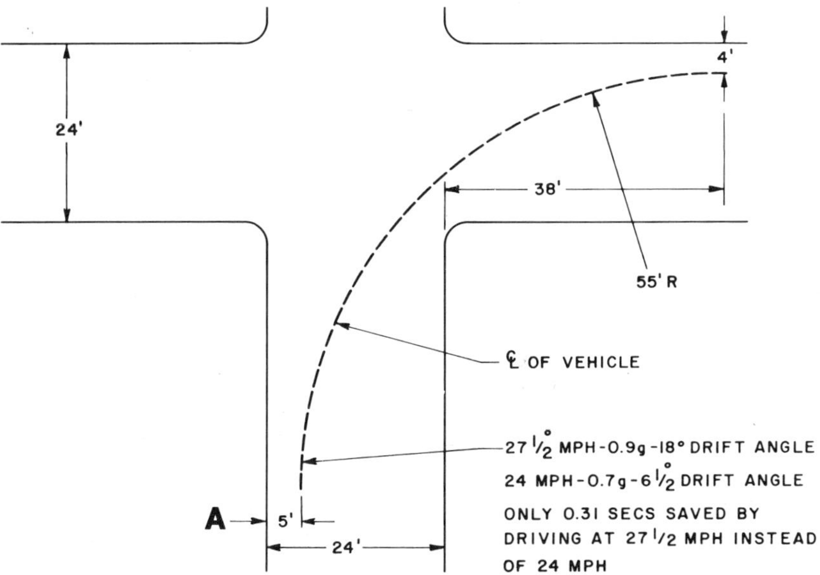

Figure 2.15. For a typical suburban intersection like this the difference between a "breakaway" speed and a safe speed is only *3½ mph.*

All the calculations and speeds are based on ideal conditions: a dry road with a high coefficient of friction, no parked vehicles so that the entire width of both streets can be used, no roadside obstacles or pedestrians that can be struck with the rear end of the vehicle that is "drifting out" on the turn, etc. For instance, with wet, bleeding asphalt, having a road coefficient of friction of 0.15, the maximum possible speed through the corner will be 12-13 mph instead of 27½ mph. On glare ice this could drop to 5-6 mph.

Let's look at coefficient of friction. It is very important to understand what friction coefficients are and how they can affect your emergency driving. Figure 2.16 illustrates how the coefficient of friction is normally defined. In the three examples a dial weight scale is attached to a 100 lbs block of rubber and a pull is applied to the scale until the block starts

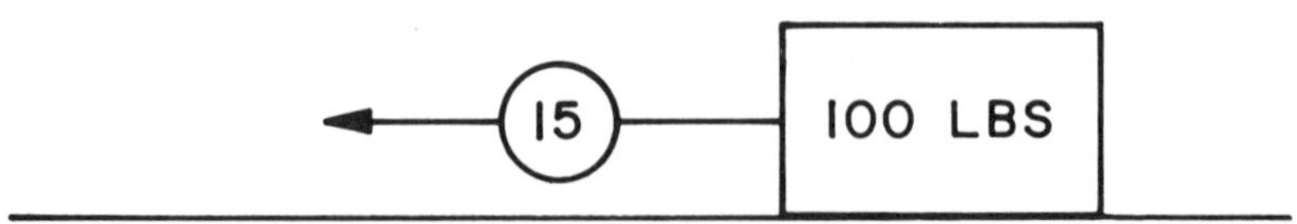

COEFFICIENT OF FRICTION $= \frac{15}{100} = .15$

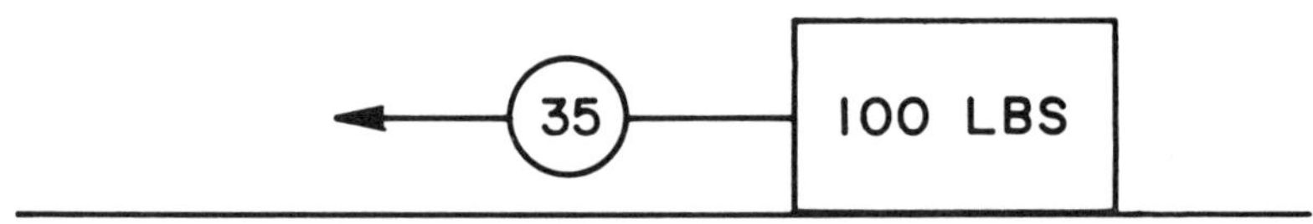

COEFFICIENT OF FRICTION $= \frac{35}{100} = .35$

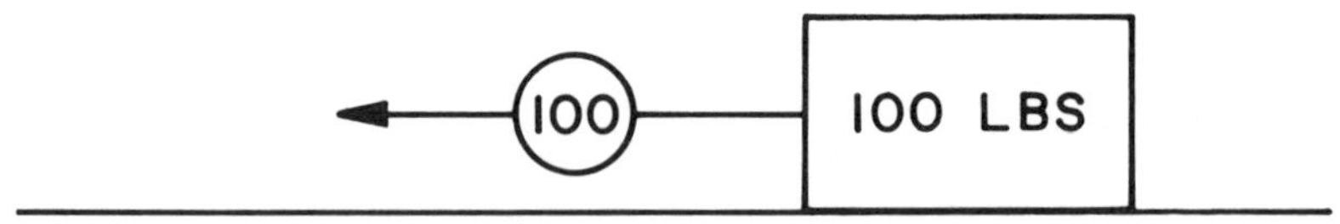

COEFFICIENT OF FRICTION $= \frac{100}{100} = 1.0$

Figure 2.16. These drawings indicate how the coefficient of friction is determined.

sliding. By reading the scale *after* the block starts sliding we can determine how much pull it requires to keep the block moving. In the first example 15 lbs are required to slide the block, so: 15/100 = .15, the coefficient of friction. If the block weighed 200 lbs the pull required to keep it moving would be: 200 (.15) = 30 lbs. In other words, the coefficient of friction multiplied by the weight of the object is the amount of pull that will be required to slide it along a given surface. In the third example, the coefficient of friction is 1.00 since the full weight of the block applied to the scale is required to keep the block moving.

Normally 1.0 is the highest coefficient of friction that the tire footprints can develop in contact with the road surface. In actual practice the road surface is seldom this abrasive and the coefficient of friction is lower. See Figure 2.17 for a range of coefficients of friction for various wet and dry road surfaces. The coefficient of friction for the Portland Cement road surface is, unfortunately, true only for relatively new concrete road surfaces. Tires rolling over concrete tend to polish it and seriously reduce the original coefficient of friction. Coefficients of friction for dry, wear polished concrete have been measured as low as .10 to .15. The highway departments of the various states normally resurface these slick surfaces with asphalt or groove them with diamond saws to increase the coefficient of friction. *Always* remember when driving on unfamiliar dry streets, that coefficients of friction can vary from .10 to .90 depending opon the age of the road and the material of construction. When in doubt slow down and avoid a possibly serious accident! In Chapter 3 the effect of friction coefficients on stopping distance is examined.

A Simulated Emergency Run

Now that some of the important points about tire performance have been covered, it is important that this knowledge be applied in determining the safest and smoothest way to

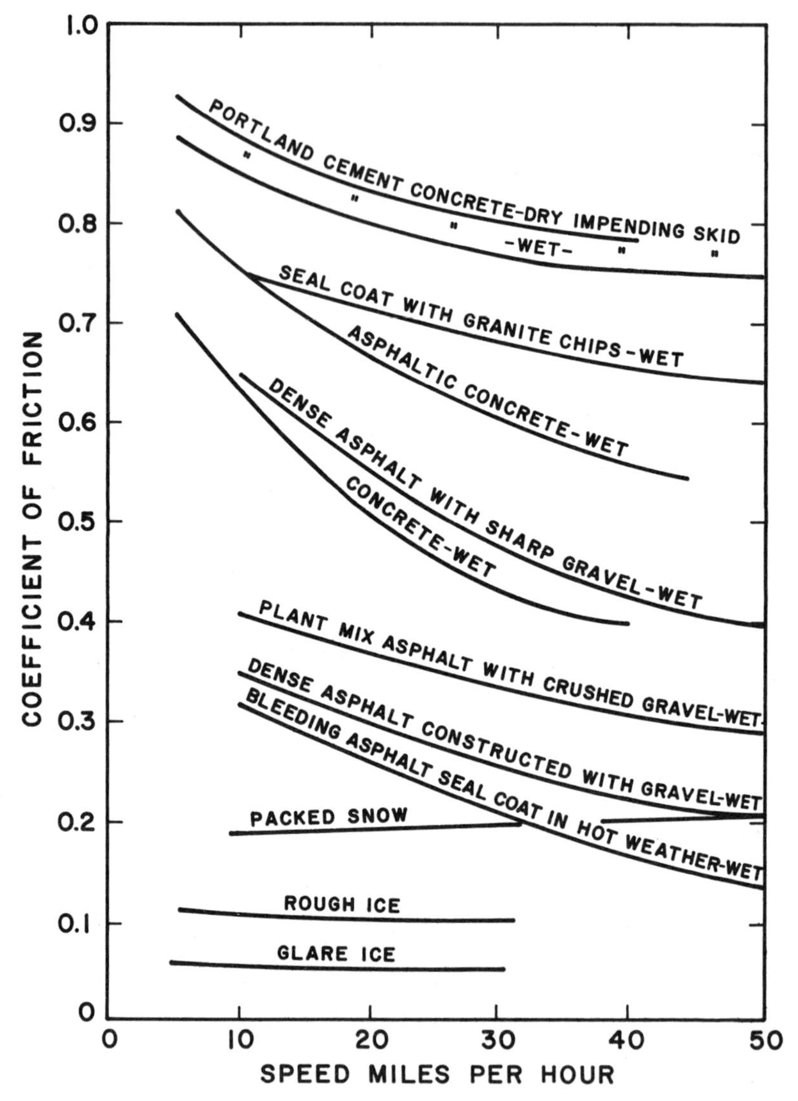

Figure 2.17. Friction coefficients vary greatly with speed, surface type and condition. (Used with permission of the Society of Automotive Engineers, Inc., Warrendale, Pa.)

drive through an exit ramp corner at emergency speeds.

Exit ramps occur in a wide variety of widths, radii, and other important factors. Therefore, a representative example has been selected. It is assumed that this is a Code 3 run and that it is desirable to maintain maximum safe speed through the turn. The turn has a 110-ft radius and is one that can be safely and comfortably entered at 36 mph. As much roadway as possible will be used so that the turn radius can remain as large as possible. As shown in Figure 2.18, the turn is started close to the left hand curb at point A. As we start our turn at the proper distance from the corner we do the following things:

1. Remove foot from the brake or accelerator.
2. Steer the vehicle smoothly toward the apex of the turn. The apex of the turn is the last part of the inside curb that can be seen from point A.
3. At point B, the apex, the vehicle should be "locked into the groove," i.e., cornering on a constant radius turn with the correct vehicle drift angle and with the vehicle as close to the inside curb as possible. Keep the vehicle close to the inside curb to allow room for increasing the turn radius by moving toward the outside curb if the vehicle starts to "breakaway."
4. On dry pavement when the vehicle is safely locked "into the groove" with the correct vehicle drift angle and the vehicle feels "comfortable" in the turn, it is permissible to start smoothly applying some power to keep up the speed. The scrubbing drag of the tires consumes lots of energy, so the vehicle will rapidly slow to a low speed unless power is applied. But apply power carefully! The cornering force on the rear tires can disappear if too much power is applied. Practice on a test course will teach you how much power you can safely apply before the rear end of the vehicle starts to move out in a high drift angle.

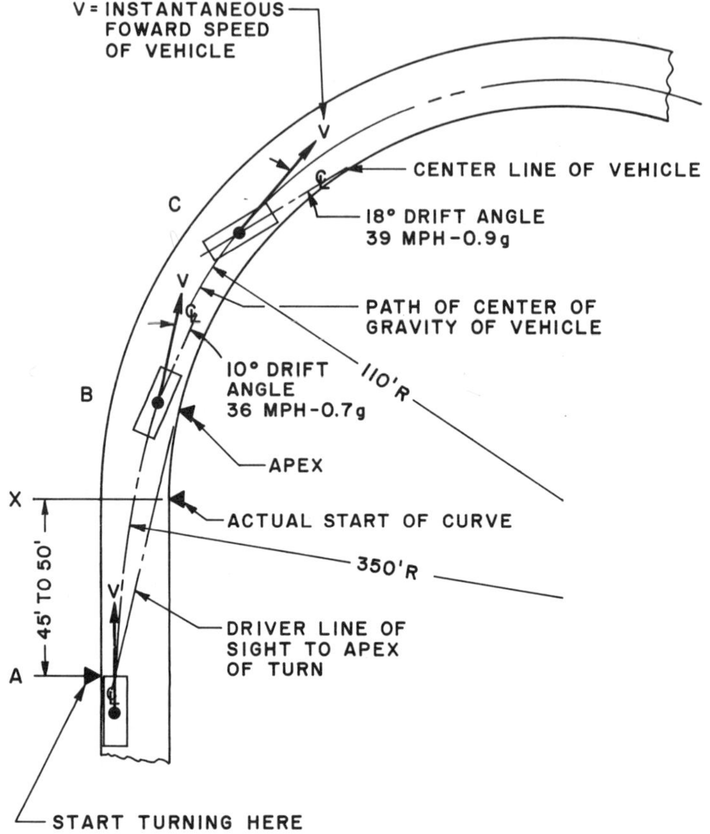

Figure 2.18. Shown here is the procedure for cornering at emergency speeds.

5. Once the vehicle is "locked into the groove" with the correct amount of throttle application, the turn has been mastered and the driver merely has to keep everything stabilized.

Once you have learned this method of cornering you will be amazed at how smoothly and effortlessly you can put the emergency vehicle through an exit ramp corner.

Note that in Figure 2.18 the vehicle is shown at point B traveling at 36 mph in a 10° drift angle with 0.7*g* centrifugal force. This is the maximum "comfortable" cornering speed and the minimum limit-of-adhesion speed. If we were able to drive the vehicle through the half circle exit ramp 3 mph faster, at 39 mph instead of 36 mph, how much time would we save? Exactly 0.51 second! We would save a half second and risk a lifetime! Is it worth it? We'll let you answer that! But you should realize it is impossible to maintain speed at an 18° drift angle because power cannot be applied without breakaway of the rear tires. So the saving in time would be possibly 0.2 second or less.

In this type of cornering we move "into the groove" as close to the inside curb as it is safe to drive. Why? Because if we have entered the corner at excessive speed or the vehicle hits a slick spot and it is necessary to increase the radius of turn to keep from losing control, we have some room to move to the outside before the outside rear tire trips on the outside curb and rolls the vehicle over. Maintain as much maneuvering room on the outside of the turn as you safely can. It could save you from a nasty roll-over if you momentarily lose control.

It should be noted that by moving to the far outside at the start of the turn (Figure 2.18) and then steering toward the apex at the proper time we are able to increase the turn radius to about 350 ft. This eases us into the turn smoothly and the change from the 350 ft radius to the 110 ft radius can also be made smoothly without any abrupt steering angle changes. Remember, always practice smooth steering unless a recovery steering correction to increase the turn radius (decrease the drift angle) must be made and that is made with a snap of the steering wheel. You will know when you have mastered the cornering technique, because your turns will be smooth and you will feel confident and "comfortable" in the turn.

In the hypothetical emergency run previously described, the exit ramp was a constant radius exit ramp. Unfortunately, they are not always constructed in this manner. The designers

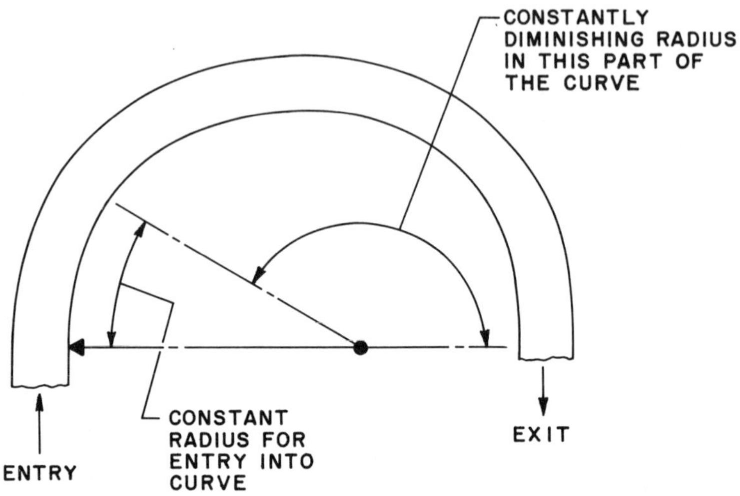

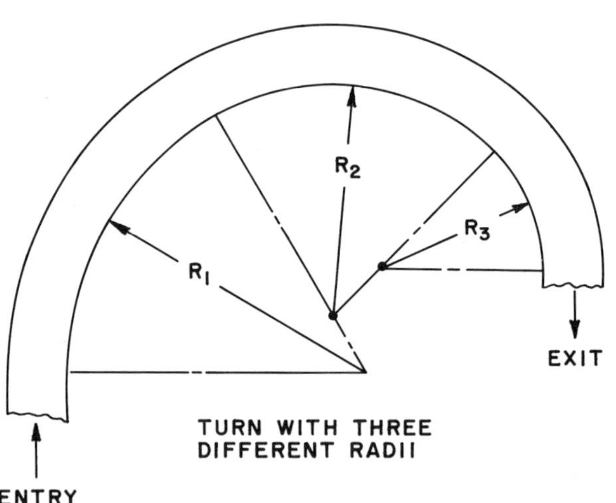

Figure 2.19. Diminishing radius turns can be designed in various ways, but all can be tricky.

at the various state highway departments often are limited by the available land so they must design a "diminishing radius turn" to fit into the area they can use. The turn starts out with a relatively large radius that allows a reasonably high, safe, entry speed but then the turn radius shortens rapidly as the vehicle penetrates into the curve. This does not affect the average, careful driver because they use the scrubbing drag of the drifting tires to slow the vehicle down to a safe speed to make the last part of the turn. But the driver who locks "into the groove," sets up the proper vehicle drift angle, and then starts applying power to maintain speed will suddenly find his speed is above the limit of adhesion for the radius available and his vehicle will leave the roadway. These ramps are quite common and can be easily identified by a series of black, greasy tire tracks at a certain point in the curve where vehicles leave the road surface in panic brake lockups.

The diminishing radius turn can be designed in various ways and two typical designs are shown in Figure 2.19. There is the spiral, with a steadily decreasing radius, and there are the turns with two or more different changes of turn radii. Either one can be deadly for the high speed driver who is not alert. It is difficult for any driver to look ahead and to decide whether the approaching curve is or is not a diminishing radius turn. It is normally necessary to first drive through the curve with the power off to be certain that you won't enter a reduced radius sector with too much speed. Play it safe on unfamiliar sections of road and live longer!

Only by understanding such factors as brake fade, reaction time, and friction coefficients, can proper braking be achieved.

3 BRAKING

Braking, although the most important function in driving a vehicle, is perhaps the least understood of all the driver functions. There are probably more incorrect "old wives tales" about braking than any other part of vehicle driving.

Instructors find it difficult to teach emergency driver trainees to execute a maximum braking effort stop because it seems to violate the years of training that taught them not to abuse the vehicle. When the trainee finally learns how to make a maximum braking effort stop, he is always surprised to learn in what a short distance the vehicle traveling at 40-50 mph, can be stopped if the pavement has a high coefficient of friction. The modern vehicle, equipped with disc brakes on the front wheels and large drum brakes on the rear wheels, has an excellent braking system.

Remember, any braking effort, whether to a full stop or just to reduce speed, should be executed as smoothly as possible. However, if it is necessary to stop in the shortest possible distance to avoid collision, it is far better to use your brakes *hard* than to subject your patient to the shock of a collision.

Brake Fade

If you have been driving any appreciable number of years you have heard of brake fade. Just what is brake fade?

Brake fade is encountered in drum brakes when excessive heat buildup in the drum causes the rubbed surface of the drum and the rubbed surface of the brake lining to heat to approximately 700°F or higher. At this temperature the bonding material of the brake lining melts and becomes a lubricant. After that, the braking force or stopping force exerted by the brakes essentially disappears. When brake fade occurs it gives the driver the eerie feeling that the vehicle is actually accelerating rather than stopping! It is a helpless feeling similar to going down a steep hill on roller skates. Fortunately, the automotive engineers have made changes in design and in materials for the linings and drums, as well as increasing the use of front disc brakes to provide the majority of the braking force.

What causes the brakes to heat up when a vehicle is stopped? Energy! A 4000 lb vehicle traveling at 55 mph represents a tremendous amount of energy that must be absorbed in stopping the vehicle. A moving body has what engineers call kinetic energy. When braking occurs, this kinetic energy is changed into heat energy, which must be absorbed by the brakes. The kinetic energy of a 4000 lb vehicle traveling at 55 mph represents enough energy to lift it over 100 feet straight up. Or, looking at the kinetic energy, if converted to heat energy, the heat energy is sufficient to heat a 20-lb anvil to almost 300°F or 5 lbs of steel to almost 900°F. All this heat energy must be absorbed by the surface of the drums in about three seconds in a panic brake stop from 55 mph. The drums are slow in absorbing this heat. You know from experience that if you turn the heat on high under a heavy iron skillet it takes almost a minute for it to get hot. What this means is that only a few pounds of each brake drum is forced to absorb all this heat energy, without cooling, during the three seconds of brake application. This can heat the surface of the brake drum to a red heat in this length of time.

There are only two ways that the red hot surface of the brake drums can cool; by conduction and by radiation. Con-

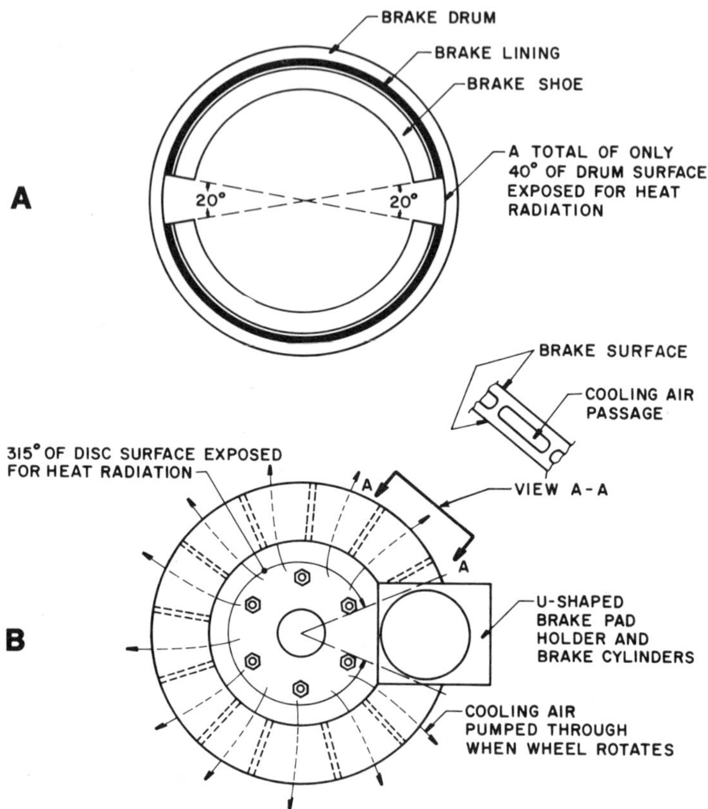

Figure 3.1. These diagrams of typical drum brakes, A, *and disc brakes,* B, *illustrate why disc brakes cool much faster.*

duction can happen two ways; the heat can be conducted to the air or conducted through the thickness of the drum. Both of these are very slow. Heat can also be given off by radiation, such as from the sun, from a blazing fire in a fire place, or from a heat lamp. This is the most rapid way of removing heat from a brake drum, but unfortunately only about 1/9 of the entire rubbed surface of the brake drum is exposed, thus allowing very little heat to be radiated (See Figure 3.1A). The portion of the drum that is covered and rubbed by the brake shoes is having energy pumped into it 8/9 of the braking time, so it is impossible for heat to radiate from the brake surface.

Disc Brakes

There are many claims about the superiority of disc brakes over drum brakes. Are the claims true? Yes, the claims are definitely true and have been proven on the test courses, race tracks, and in daily usage. Disc brakes or "spot brakes" were used on World War II aircraft to provide fast, fade-free braking. In the fifties the British started installing them on their Grand Prix racing cars. The superior braking permitted them to start braking later as they aproached each turn. This saved them seconds on each lap and they won races because of the improved brakes. The Italians evidently not wanting to use British made disc brakes on their racing cars were the last to change over. They designed some extremely sophisticated drum brakes in an attempt to match disc brake performance but were forced to admit defeat and use disc brakes to stay competitive. Foreign made sport cars and luxury sedans installed disc brakes in the late fifties but U.S. vehicle manufacturers resisted stubbornly until the late sixties and early seventies before finally changing over to this improved design.

Four wheel disc brakes provide the ideal braking system but only the highest priced sports cars and luxury cars have such a system. Most cars use the discs only in front. There are three good reasons for this: (1) approximately 65% of the braking effort comes from the front wheels (2) it is difficult and expensive to design a parking (emergency) brake into a disc brake (3) discs are more expensive than drum brakes and the manufacturers believe it is not "cost effective" to install them on the rear.

With respect to the difficulty of cooling the inside surface of a brake drum, the disc brake offers an outstanding design advantage over the drum brake. As Figure 3.1B indicates, at least 85% of the disc brake's rubbed surface is exposed so that heat can be radiated away from it. The better disc brakes are designed with air-cooling passages inside the drum, as shown in Figure 3.1B. This helps prevent heat buildup in the disc on repeated applications. Remember, the heat is slow to penetrate into the disc material, therefore it is slow in leaving the material of the disc. The superior cooling from radiation and from being exposed to air cooling is what gives the disc brake its improved performance over the drum brake. In contrast, the drum brake is sealed off so it only gets coling air on the outside surface of the drum and has little chance for losing heat by radiation except to the sealed-off interior. As said previously, disc brakes have forced drum brakes off all racing vehicles, the most severe test of braking performance!

Friction Coefficients and Stopping Distance

For a vehicle to stop or reduce its speed there must be a transfer of force through the tire footprints to the ground just as there is in a cornering maneuver. In Chapter 2 we learned that the force that a tire can develop in contact with the road surface is dependent upon the coefficient of friction (Figures 2.16 and 2.17). Figure 2.17 indicates the driver of an emergency vehicle can meet a wide range of road conditions with a corresponding wide range of coefficients of friction. With good brakes a vehicle's stopping distance is completely dependent upon the coefficient of friction, the force the tires can develop in gripping the road surface. The formula to calculate stopping distance is

$$S = V^2/2\mu g \tag{3.1}$$

where

S = Stopping distance (ft)
V = Velocity (ft/sec)
μ = Coefficient of friction
g = Acceleration of gravity, (32.16 ft/sec^2)

It can be seen that if μ, the coefficient of friction, is reduced, then S, the stopping distance, will be increased. As an example, let's calculate the minimum stopping distance from 55 mph on a dry Portland Cement surface with an average coefficient of friction of 0.8.

V = 55 mph = 80.67 ft/sec
μ = 0.8

Therefore

$$S = (80.67)^2/2(0.8)(32.16) = 126.5 \text{ ft}$$

Suppose the stop from 55 mph must be made on glare ice with a coefficient of friction of 0.05.

$$S = (80.67)^2/2(0.05)(32.16) = 2023 \text{ ft (.38 miles)}$$

It will take 16 times as far to stop on glare ice as on a dry Portland cement surface.

Figure 3.2 shows the *minimum* stopping distances for a range of speeds on various road surfaces. These minimum distances are calculated on the basis that the driver is highly skilled in the use of the vehicle brakes and that he can apply the brakes in the most efficient manner for the road surface involved. Actually few drivers are this talented so the actual stopping distance will normally be greater than that shown in Figure 3.2. However, this chart indicates how important the

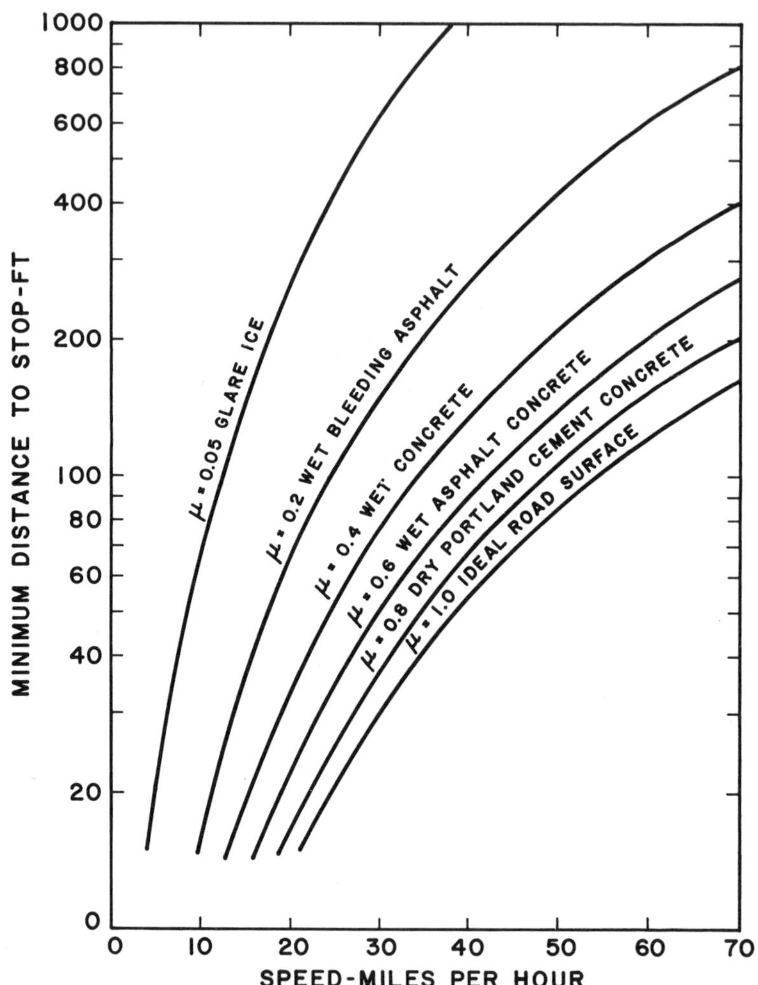

Figure 3.2. Depending upon surface friction coefficient, minimum stopping distances vary greatly with speed. (Used with permission of the Society of Automotive Engineers, Inc., Warrendale, Pa.)

condition of the road surface can be. For instance, at 38.5 mph it is possible to stop in 62 ft on dry Portland Cement concrete while it requires 1000 ft on glare ice.

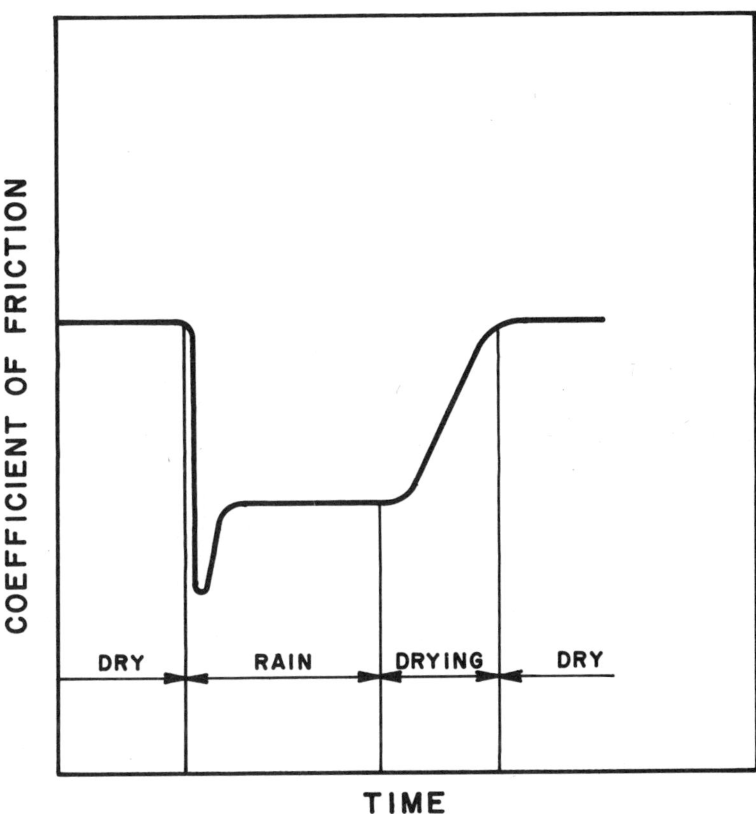

Figure 3.3. This graph shows the coefficient of friction of a typical road surface before, during, and after a rain.

Figure 3.3 illustrates how the friction coefficient of a typical road surface is affected before, during, and after a rain. The lowest coefficient of friction, shown in Figure 3.3 as a sharp dip, occurs shortly after the rain begins. This is caused by the rain mixing with dirt and oil on the road surface to form a slick film. As the rain continues, the film is washed away and the friction coefficient returns to a stable value. This change in the friction coefficient just after the start of the rain can easily add another 200-225 ft of stopping distance at 55 mph. To re-

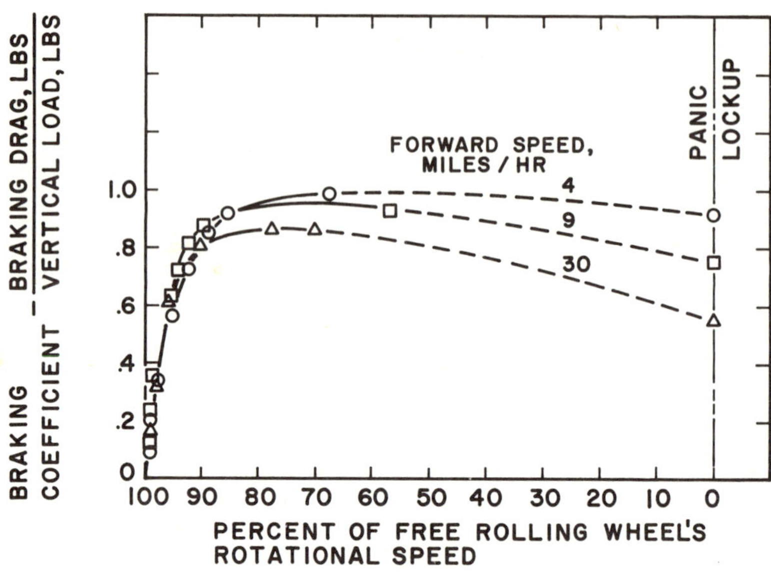

Figure 3.4. Braking coefficient vs percent of free rolling wheel's rotational speed. (Used with permission of the Society of Automotive Engineers, Inc., Warrendale, Pa.)

tain the same stopping distance it would be necessary to slow down to 30-35 mph. When the pavement gets wet, slow down and live!

How heavily must we apply the brakes to obtain the maximum braking drag to stop in the shortest distance? This is the hardest lesson for the student emergency vehicle driver to learn. It is still a good practice to use brakes moderately but when an emergency stop must be made to avoid a collision then a little tread rubber and attracting unwanted attention is a cheap price to pay. Figure 3.4 shows how much the tire must slide to develop maximum braking force. If the wheel stops turning in a panic lockup the braking force decreases because localized heating of the tire creates a molten layer of rubber. To obtain maximum braking effort the tire must rotate sufficiently to keep putting cooler rubber on the road surface.

Therefore, we must avoid "locking up" the brakes but still apply them heavily enough to cause the tires to protest loudly and to "lay a little rubber on the road." A panic lockup not only reduces the braking force but it tends to start loss of control. The center of gravity of the vehicle will move forward in a straight line, with panic lockup, regardless of the steering angle of the front wheels, and the vehicle may rotate 15-20° in one direction or another. This could mean striking other cars in adjacent lanes of traffic. When the student driver finally learns how to "come down hard" on the brakes without a panic lockup, he is always amazed at how the vehicle can be stopped in such a short distance without losing control. It takes practice to develop the driver-vehicle closed loop system feedback (Figure 1.1) needed to get the correct "seat-of-the-pants" feel on maximum braking effort.

Before leaving the subject of braking it will be helpful to remind the student that heavy braking reduces the available cornering force. Heavy braking in a turn will cause the vehicle to leave the highway in a straight line. This is why we see the straight or slightly curved black tire skidmarks leaving the expressway exit ramp curves—someone applied their brakes too heavily in the curve!

The human element enters into the stopping distance by way of the reaction time. The reaction time is the time required for the driver to see the need for a quick stop, decide to stop, lift his foot off the acclerator, put his foot on the brake, and then apply enough push to the brake to start stopping the vehicle. The average human can accomplish all of this in approximately 3/4 of a second. Actually there may be a considerable difference between different persons depending upon their training, their physical coordination, their age, their agility, and other factors. Stirling Moss, the famous racing driver, was an unusual person with a reaction time of 0.2 second. Some of the elderly drivers on the road may have a reaction time of two seconds or more. A slow reaction time may mean the difference between a serious crash and a safe stop. During the entire time the braking foot is moving toward the brake pedal the vehicle is rapidly shortening the available braking distance. At 55 mph the vehicle is traveling at 80.7 ft/sec. If the driver has an average reaction time of 3/4 of a second the vehicle will have moved 60.5 ft before braking can be started. It was calculated previously that it would take 126.5 ft to stop from 55 mph with a dry concrete road surface. The 60.5 ft of reaction time travel has added an extra 48% to our overall stopping distance for a total of 187 ft.

Reaction time is the controlling factor in maintaining a safe following distance. Figure 3.5 shows two vehicles traveling along the highway at 55 mph. Vehicle *Y* starts a maximum braking effort when its rear bumper is at point *B*. How far should vehicle *X* be behind vehicle *Y* to avoid running into the back of vehicle *Y*? Since the driver of vehicle *X* is traveling at 80.7 ft/sec and is assumed to have a reaction time of .75 second, vehicle *X* will travel (.75 sec) (80.7 ft/sec) = 60.5 ft. Therefore, point *A* must be at least 60.5 ft behind point *B* if vehicle *X* is to avoid hitting the vehicle ahead. This, of course, assumes that the two vehicles can stop in exactly the same distance from 55 mph. Theoretically, the bumper of vehicle *X* should just touch the bumper of vehicle *Y* as they finally come to a stop if the minimum following distance is maintained. For mental calculation it is roughly equal in feet to the speed in mph plus 10%; i.e., at 55 mph it is equal to 55 + 5.5 = 60.5 ft or roughly three vehicle lengths. Now it should be emphasized that this is a *red line* minimum following distance. Any reduction in this minimum following distance constitutes a reckless form of "tailgating". The slightest inattention or slowdown in reaction time will result in a crash when following close. Figure 3.6 illustrates two sets of results when the following vehicle, (*X*), neglects to brake or is one second slower than normal in braking when the lead vehicle, (*Y*), performs a maximum effort braking stop. With no braking the closing speed at impact between the two vehicles is 32.5 mph and the collision occurs in 2⅓ seconds after vehicle *Y* starts to brake. If the

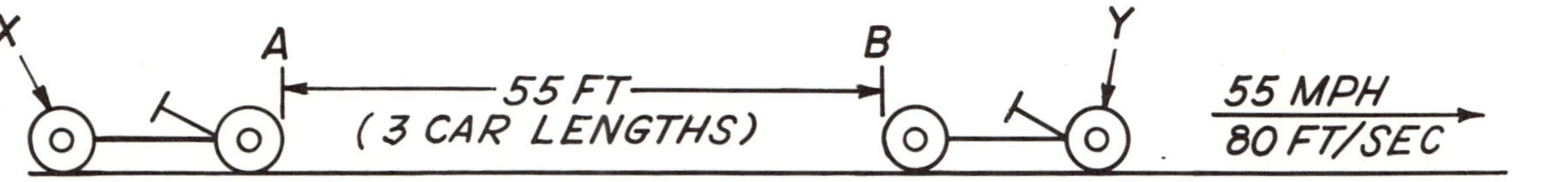

ONE FOOT PER MPH IS THE ABSOLUTE MINIMUM FOLLOWING DISTANCE:

REACTION TIME: 0.69 SECONDS
VELOCITY AT 55 MPH: 80 FT/SEC
0.69 X 80 = 55 FT

CAR "B" WILL TRAVEL 55 FT BEFORE DRIVER CAN START APPLYING HIS BRAKE.

RECOMMENDED FOLLOWING DISTANCE:
ONE CAR LENGTH FOR EACH 10 MPH
55 MPH = 5½ CAR LENGTHS

Figure 3.5. The best way to avoid collisions is to maintain proper distance between your vehicle and another's.

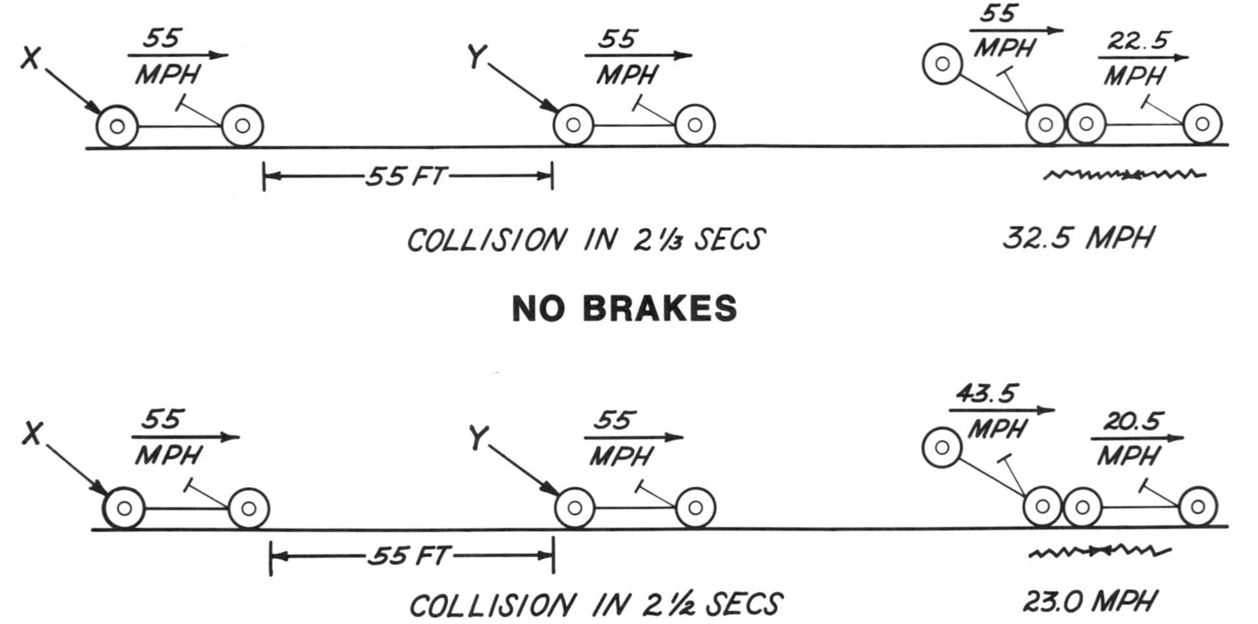

Figure 3.6. Shown here are collision speeds for negligently driven following vehicles.

driver of vehicle *X* is one second slow on reaction (he takes 1¾ seconds to brake), then the closing speed at impact will be 23 mph and the collision will occur 2½ seconds after vehicle *Y* starts to brake. Therefore, if you are one second slow in braking due to carelessness or inattention, the resultant crash is going to be almost as serious as if you don't brake at all! This is another good reason why 100% attention to the road ahead is mandatory for the emergency vehicle driver.

You have been told of the dangers of heavy braking in a turn but it is necessary now to tell you when, how, and why brakes can be applied safely in approaching an unexpected tight corner. On a Code 3 run on unfamiliar roads there will probably be a time when you will suddenly realize you are rapidly approaching a tight curve or expressway exit ramp at a speed that is too fast for safe cornering. In general the cornering procedure should follow the procedure outlined previously for emergency speed cornering illustrated in Figure 2.18. Referring now to Figure 3.7, maximum effort braking should be used as quickly as possible and applied right up to point *A*. If it is a clear two way street or a one way exit ramp, ease the vehicle to the outside of the curve to provide the maximum possible radius as you start into the turn. After reaching point *A* the brakes must be progressively released to increase cornering force as point *B* is approached. Before reaching point *B* the brakes must be fully released and the vehicle should be free rolling so that the maximum possible drift angle can be used at point *B* if it is required because of excessive entry speed. If the vehicle is at the maximum possible drift angle it will be developing all the drag or brake force possible under the circumstances while still maintaining the maximum possible cornering force. From point *B* on there is *no need for brake application* to help maintain the vehicle on the road. If you have slowed the vehicle enough to stabilize it and set up a drift angle and maintain it past point *B*—Congratulations! If you are moving too fast or have failed to establish enough cornering force as you pass point *B* the author extends his con-

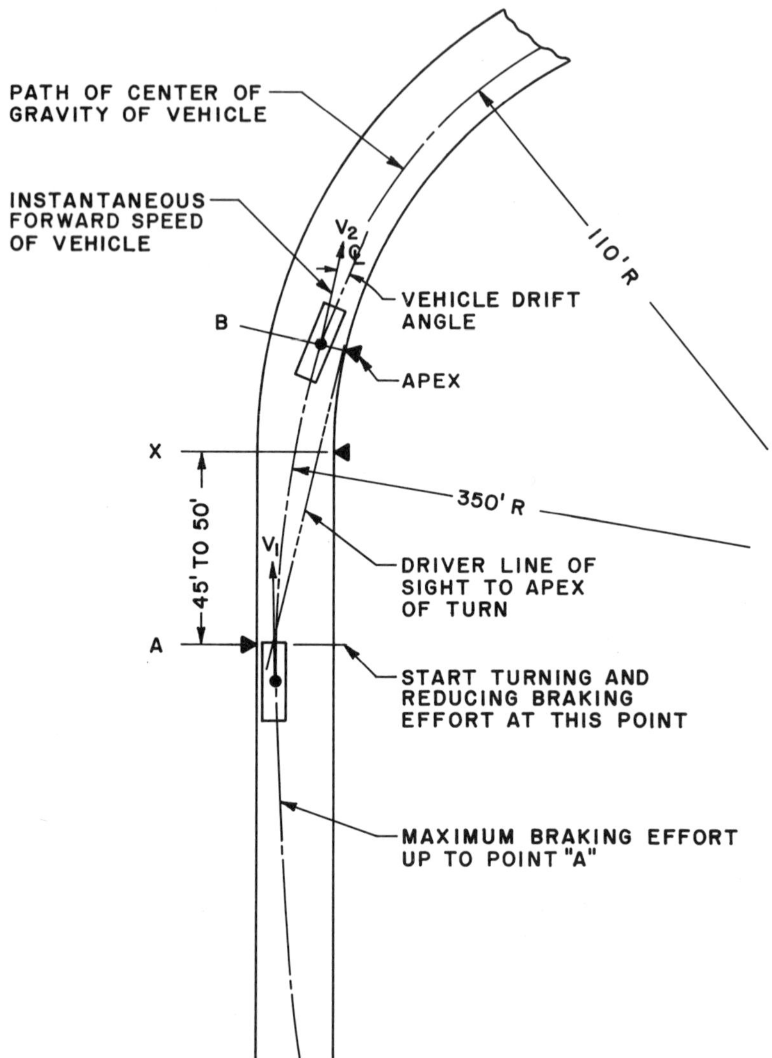

Figure 3.7. Hard braking for an unexpected turn is tricky because it requires achieving the maximum possible drift angle without losing cornering force.

dolences and hopes you survive leaving the roadway. In Chapter 5 the correct technique for leaving the roadway is examined.

There is a persistent old wives' tale about the advantages of "pumping" the brakes in a high speed emergency stop. Between 10 and 20 years ago, before brakes and brake material were improved, this was one way to avoid brake fade. Taking your foot off the brake for a short time before reapplying them heavily permitted some of the surface heat to radiate off the inner drum surface and thereby reduce the tendency to fade. If the brakes would normally fade on an emergency braking stop from 60-70 mph then "pumping" would produce a shorter stopping distance. With the advent of disc brakes, improved brake material and drums, and the resultant disappearance of brake fade, the rules of the game have now changed. The shortest stopping distance is obtained by a steady, heavy brake application with a 15% slowdown in rotational speed from a free rolling tire. When the foot is not applying braking pressure during "pumping" the tire is free rolling and moving ahead unchecked toward the danger in the road ahead. A race driver uses a steady heavy application of brakes to get the speed down from perhaps 150 mph to a curve entry speed of 40 mph. *They do not pump their brakes*!

The anti-skid braking devices on the market pump the brakes at perhaps 10 times per second, far faster than a human could possibly do it. Yet the stopping distance with these devices is increased over what a *skilled* driver could do under the same conditions. The anti-skid devices are excellent for the average driver who has never practiced emergency braking stops. For the average unskilled driver the resultant stop is undoubtedly shorter and far safer under adverse road conditions with the anti-skid device. By way of explanation the normal anti-skid braking device senses wheel rotation and when the wheel starts to lock-up in a skid the braking pressure is momentarily released until the wheel rotation starts up again and then the brakes are reapplied until the wheel again approaches lock-up. Unfortunately, the electronics that do this cannot adjust the brake pressure to obtain the 15% slowdown in rotation that the skilled driver can obtain. The electronics must do it with an on-off technique that is less than optimum for the skilled driver.

Some highly sophisticated anti-skid systems that permit heavy brake application with continuous braking without wheel lockup have been proposed and are in the development stage. These will be available in the future but they will not be inexpensive. Meanwhile you must learn to do now what the complicated "black box" will do for you in an emergency stop on future vehicle designs.

The effect of tire conditions and characteristics on vehicle handling is phenomenal.

4
TIRE DESIGN

As an emergency vehicle driver you should understand the differences between the three tire designs; radial ply, cross-bias ply and cross-bias ply belted. Probably the radial ply tire will be virtually the only quality tire design to be manufactured in the future. Manufacturers of "cheapies", tires built in the less expensive cross-bias ply design, may find that future Department of Transportation performance specifications can be met economically only by radial ply tires.

Figure 4.1 illustrates the difference in construction details between the radial ply tire and the cross-bias ply tires. Both tires have wire reinforcement in the beads. The radial ply tire has walls reinforced with cords strung radially from bead to bead. In passenger car tires this is normally limited to two layers of cord giving the tire a smoother ride at low speeds. In contrast, the cross-bias ply tire has two to four layers of cord laid in a cross-biased lattice structure. The cords are laid in such a way to form an angle of about 33° with the circumference of the tire. Both tire designs use a rubber lining to cover the fabric casing and contain the air, both designs are covered outside with rubber for protection against wear and damage, and both designs enclose the reinforcing bead wires within an overlap of the casing fabric, often with additional

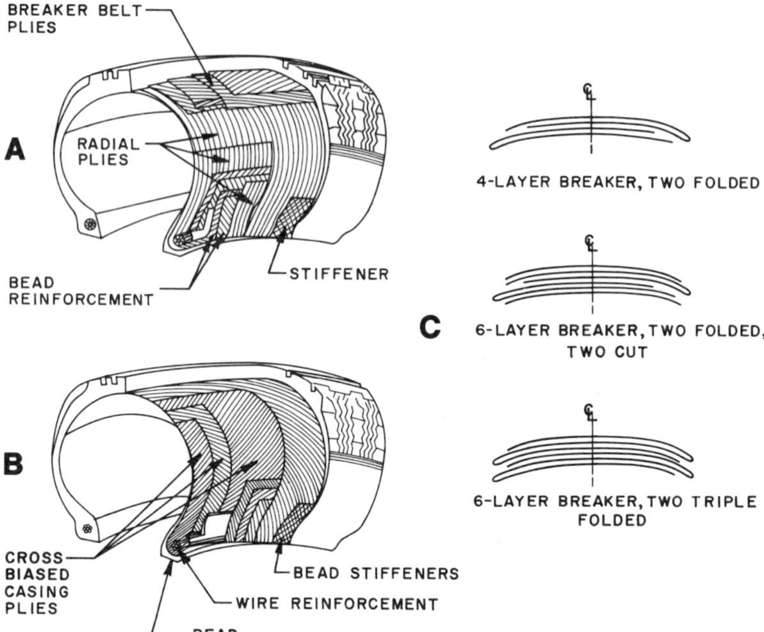

Figure 4.1. Shown here are the construction details of a radial tire, A, *and a cross-biased ply tire,* B. *Illustrated at* C *are the types of breakers that are used in radial tires.*

reinforcing strips of cross-biased fabric extending a short way up the sidewalls.

In a "true" radial ply tire there is a rigid breaker, or belt, of relatively inextensible fabric that girdles the outer circumference of the casing just below the tread. The breaker belt is composed of 2 or 3 layers of steel cords arranged at angles for strength and tread stability. Common layup angles with respect to the circumference of the tire are +90° for 3-layer construction and +16° and −16° for 2-layer belts. The steel cords are multistrand cables of hairlike wires for flexibility. A typical cord has 12 strands of 0.0059 inch diameter wire (about twice the thickness of a human hair), built up to a total of

0.030 inch in cord diameter with a breaking strength of 100 lbs or more.

Passenger car radial ply tires are usually built of 1-4 radial plys of rayon, nylon, or other textiles. Breakers are built of either 2 layers of steel cords or 4-6 layers of textile cords. In the 4-layer textile breaker the cords are usually angled 12-20° to the tire circumference. The 4 layers are doubled one over another in pairs as shown in Figure 4.1C. The 6 layers are folded in threes or with two folded over and two cut. The folding increases the stiffness of the breaker belt at the edge to achieve maximum stability and rigidity. The textile cords used in the breaker belt are thicker than those used in the radial portion of the casing and have a lower elongation and twist, and, therefore, a much greater stiffness.

Why does the increased stiffness of the steel or textile belt under the tread of a radial ply tire provide improved performance? To answer that it is necessary to examine Figure 4.2 where we see a typical cross-biased tire footprint at A and a typical steel belted radial ply tire footprint at B. The tires are being viewed from below as they would appear if they were rolling across a glass plate. For clarity the shape of the tread in the footprints is exaggerated in each instance.

The movement of the tread in the cross-biased tire's footprint is known in automotive circles as "squirming". As the tire in Figure 4.2A rolls forward and a spot on the tread, X, enters the footprint area it is pushed upward radially toward the center of the wheel by the weight of the vehicle. It has been shoved in radially a maximum amount when it reaches X'. There is a fixed length of material from one bead to the other so when X is shoved in radially the tendency is for the excess material to force the ribs to close up because the construction of the tire under the tread is not sufficiently resistant to prevent this compression of the tread. With lower inflation pressures this is exaggerated since there is a greater radial movement of the tread toward the center of the wheel. It can be seen that point X, in rib 1, in moving through the footprint

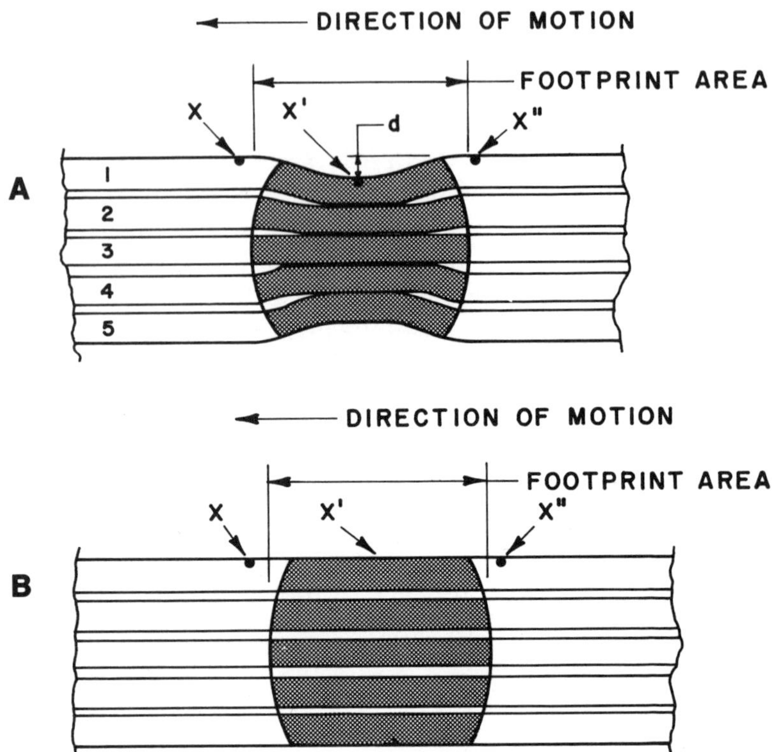

Figure 4.2. A shows how "squirming" reduces the footprint area of a typical cross-biased tire, while radial footprint areas, B, *are unaffected because of their rigid construction.*

to X' must slide or skid through the distance d. All points across rib 1 at point X' skid approximately the same amount. As the tire rolls forward and X' moves through the tire footprint to X'', then X' must skid back through the same distance d. The same thing happens on rib 5.

Corresponding points on ribs 2 and 4 move approximately half as far as points on ribs 1 and 5. Rib 3 is the only rib that does not experience continuous sliding through the tire footprint area.

In contrast the steel belted radial ply tire's belt under the tread is highly resistant to compression and the various points on the tread roll through the footprint area with little or no skidding, sliding, or squirming. As seen in Figure 4.2B point X moves to X' and then X'' in a straight line. The "excess" material caused by the radial movement of the tread toward the center of wheel must go somewhere, so the sidewalls of the radial ply tire bulge. This explains why radial ply tires look underinflated with "cheeky" sidewalls.

The elimination or almost complete reduction of "squirming" in a radial ply tire explains a number of its favorable characteristics as compared to a cross-biased tire.

Adhesion

Skidding reduces the effective coefficient of friction between the tire and the road surface in both wet and dry road conditions. Since most of the footprint area of a cross-bias ply tire is always skidding, it stands to reason that the "locked-in" footprint area of a steel belted radial ply tire will develop greater adhesion to the road surface, particularly on wet and icy surfaces. See Figure 4.3. Steel belted radial ply tires have an almost unbelievable adhesion in glare ice conditions.

Cornering Force

A steel belted radial or textile belted radial develops cornering force far more rapidly at low drift angles than the cross-bias tire. It does not develop a higher *maximum* cornering force (see Figure 4.4) than a cross-bias tire, because at the drift angle for *maximum* cornering force the entire footprint is skidding so the absence of "squirming" with a steel belted radial cannot be felt. Maximum cornering force for a radial tire occurs at a much lower drift angle than on the cross-bias tire. However, maximum cornering force on a radial begins to

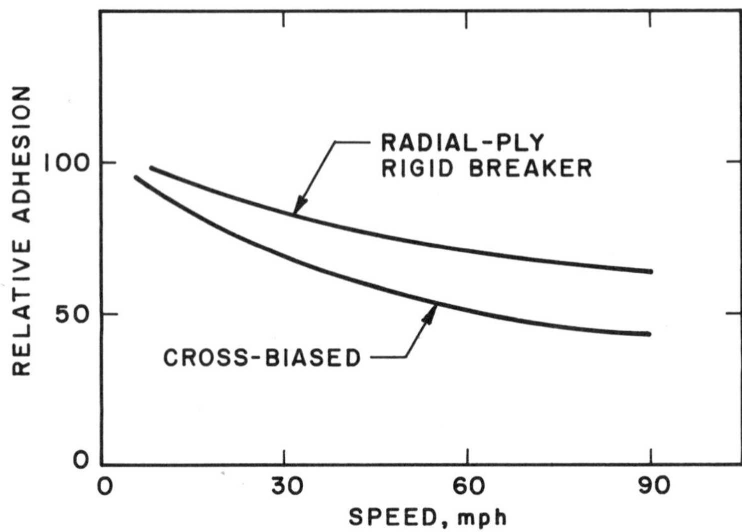

Figure 4.3. Relative adhesion vs speed of cross-biased ply and radial ply tires on a wet road surface.

drop quickly once the drift angle is increased beyond the optimum for maximum cornering force. In contrast, the cross-bias tire and the textile breaker radial have rather broad plateaus of maximum cornering force. What this means is that when cornering at the limit of adhesion with a steel belted radial it is difficult to determine that the vehicle is borderline "breakaway". With a cross-bias or textile breaker tire the tire will "warn" you that you are approaching the limit of adhesion and will allow the vehicle to move into a higher drift angle to increase the drag force and scrub off excess speed safely. Once the drift angle for maximum cornering force is passed on a steel belted radial the cornering force drops rapidly and a spin-out is almost impossible to prevent. So, the steel belted radial is not advised for the inexperienced driver to attempt maximum speed cornering! In Chapter 2 we determined that only a small amount of time could be saved in a corner by limit of adhesion cornering so the best technique is to play it safe in cornering with steel belted radials. This is the only *major* disadvantage that can be overlooked in weighing the merits of the steel belted radial. Notice it says overlooked but not forgotten. *Never forget* that a steel belted radial will stay locked into a turn as though you are traveling on a set of steel rails, but if you push them too far they will "let go" too suddenly for you to recover control!

Steering Response

Note in Figure 4.4 the sharp increase of cornering force as the drift angle increases on the radial ply tire as compared to the bias ply tire. This increases agility and quickness of steering that could provide the margin of safety in an evasive maneuver. Combined with this is the short "lag" in cornering force development on a steel belted radial ply tire as compared to a bias ply. The increased lateral stiffness of a steel belted radial provides virtually instantaneous response to a steering correction. Both of these factors provide a greatly improved factor of safety over conventional tires.

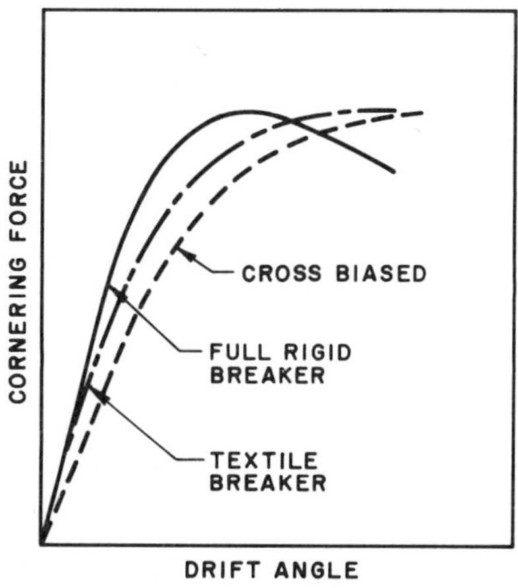

Figure 4.4. Developing greater cornering force more quickly, as indicated by this graph, is another advantage of radial tires (full rigid breaker and textile breaker) over cross-biased ply tires.

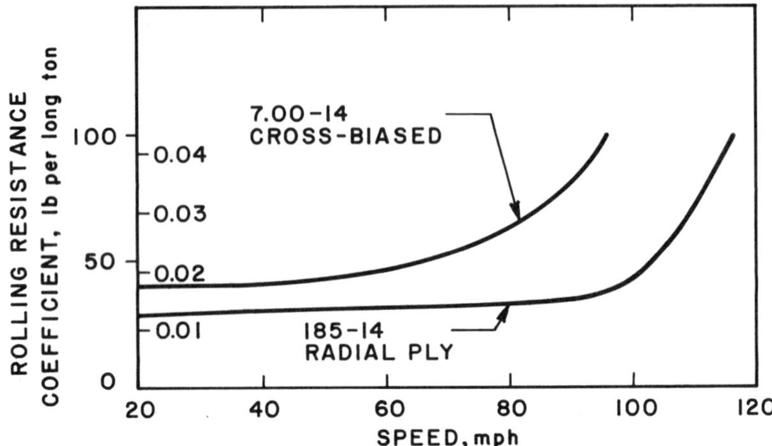

Figure 4.5. The rolling resistance data for equivalent radial ply and cross-biased tires at various speeds clearly indicates the economic advantages of radial tires. (Used with permission of the Society of Automotive Engineers, Inc., Warrendale, Pa.)

Rolling Resistance

In these days of the "energy crunch" and high fuel costs it is highly desirable to take advantage of any saving in fuel that can be realized. Note in Figure 4.5 that the rolling resistance of a radial ply tire at 55 mph is only two thirds the resistance of a cross-bias ply tire. The saving in fuel cost in 40,000 miles of emergency driving as a result of the reduced rolling resistance of the steel belted radial will normally pay for the tire.

Increased Tire Mileage

The author, in driving steel belted radials on his personal vehicles for over 350,000 miles, has experienced from 2-2½ times greater mileage with steel belted radials than with cross-bias ply tires. Therefore, just from a replacement basis alone the steel belted radials are a bargain at almost twice the price of a cross-biased tire.

Tire Ripple

Before leaving the subject of tires it will be desirable to discuss tire "ripple" at high speeds. This is a phenomenon essentially unknown to the average driver. If the average driver experiences and survives a high speed blowout caused by ripple he would never realize the cause. Figure 4.6 illustrates the deflection of a loaded tire at slow speeds in contact with a rigid road surface. There is deflection, *H* of the center of the footprint *X* toward the axis of the wheel. As the tire rolls forward the internal pressure in the tire pushes the point *X* that was the center of the footprint out toward the static outer circumference of the tire. The radial outward movement of *X* at high speed is very rapid. The rapid movement of *X* radially outward does not stop at the static outer circumference of the tire. Instead there is an "overshoot" and *X* carries out beyond

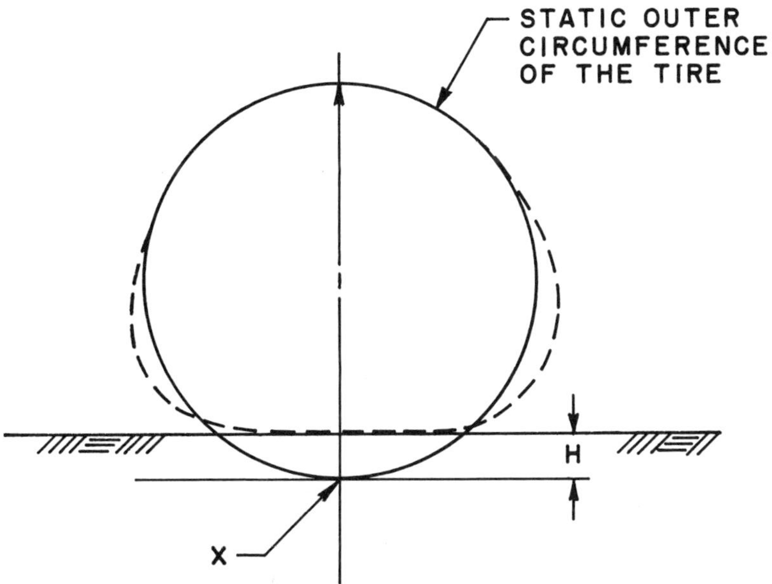

Figure 4.6. The deflection of a flexible tire caused by its intersection with a rigid road surface results in tire ripple at higher speeds.

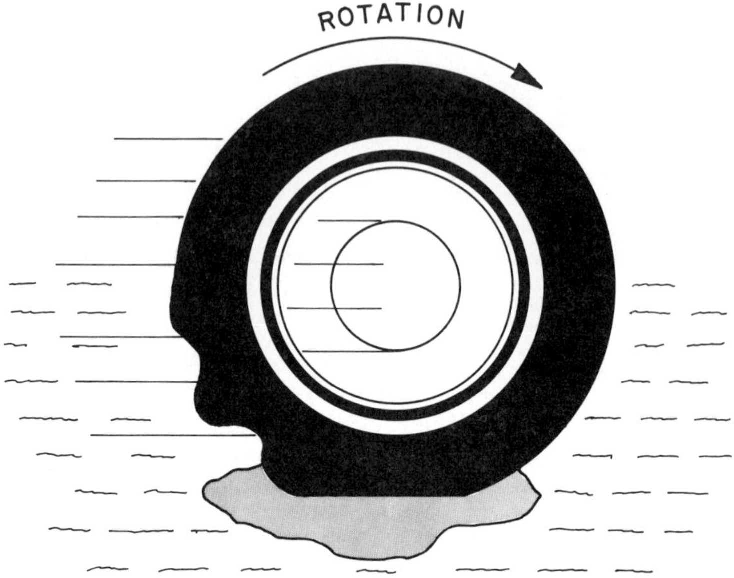

Figure 4.7. This is an exaggerated view of how tire ripple appears at high speed.

the outer circumference. It then starts back in again and moves inward beyond the static point. This is similar to the lateral vibration of a screen door spring when displaced to one side and released. This vibration is shown in Figure 4.7. This is what engineers call a "standing wave" because at any given speed, when the ripple starts, the "humps and bumps" are always in the same position. They will move their position as speed is increased or decreased.

Tire ripple starts in a cross-bias ply passenger vehicle tire at about 80 mph and gets progressively worse as speed is increased. The dangerous part of tire ripple is the rapid buildup of heat. Each time the tire revolves it is as though the tread is being run through a set of rollers. All of us know that by bending a piece of rubber back and forth rapidly that the rubber heats up. At 100 mph, tire ripple can produce temperatures high enough to cause separation of the tread from the tire carcass and separation of the plys. A high speed blowout can occur in as short a time as 3-5 minutes.

"Off-the shelf" passenger vehicle tires are not designed nor manufactured to be run at continuous high speed. Police special tires and certified racing tires are designed for continuous high speed operation without significant tire ripple and overheating. Any driver operating a passenger vehicle with production grade tires at sustained speeds of 100 mph is playing a deadly game of Russian roulette!

Figure 4.8 shows a view of the high speed ripple as viewed from behind the tire. Note that tire tread is vibrating laterally as well as radially as shown in Figure 4.6. It is understandable how the tire overheats so rapidly.

High quality steel belted radials resist tire ripple and have been accepted in sports car racing as a racing tire. Higher tire

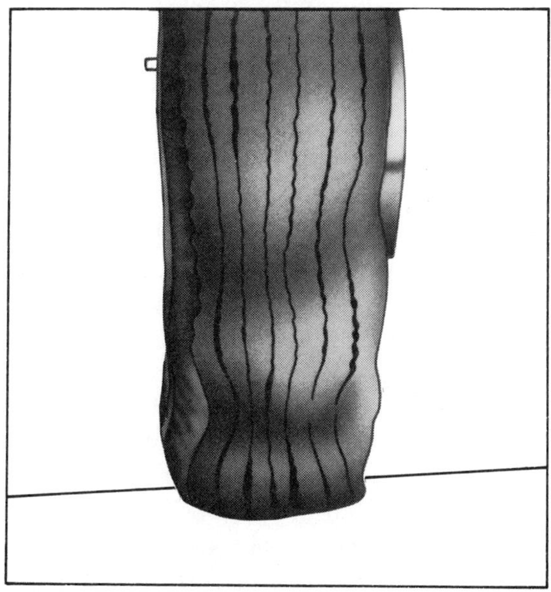

Figure 4.8. Tire ripple is also a lateral movement as shown in this rear view of a tire.

inflation pressure increases the speed for dangerous tire ripple due to the reduced deflection or radial displacement of the tread.

Tire Inflation and Its Effect on Vehicle Performance

Many different factors must be studied and understood as to how each affects cornering, braking, or even "straight ahead" highway driving. Because it is impossible to study and understand all these factors simultaneously, it is necessary to study each factor separately and determine how it affects what we have already learned. This is the case with tire inflation pressure. Unfortunately, only a small number of drivers on the road understand the tremendous effect proper tire inflation pressure can have on vehicle handling. Also, it is unfortunate that the U.S. vehicle manufacturers 10-14 years ago recommended tire inflation pressures far too low for maximum steering response and overall ease of handling. It can only be assumed that this was prompted by a desire to give the buying public "a soft ride" and to minimize the road noise and vibrations transmitted to the vehicle body by the tires. The low tire inflation pressures waste fuel due to increased rolling resistance, increase tire wear, and seriously reduce the potential steering response of the vehicles. There is excessive roll-under of the tires in tight cornering (see Figure 4.9) if passenger vehicle tires are inflated to 26 psi or lower.

The photos in Figure 4.9 are blowups from high speed 16 mm film taken at 1000 frames/second by a camera mounted ahead of the outside front wheel, the heavily loaded wheel. The turn was approximately the radius of an average highway exit ramp. The vehicle was driven through the turn at about 40 mph. In addition to the excessive roll-under of the tire at 24 psi and lower, note the significant increase in steering angle required at all pressures below 32 psi. A bias ply passenger vehicle tire normally develops its maximum cornering force at 36

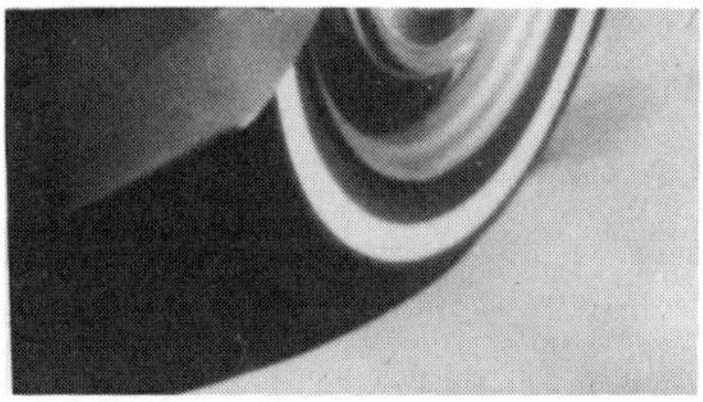

40 PSI

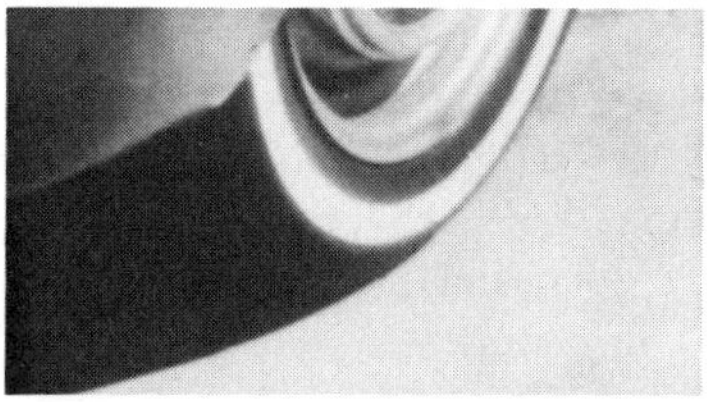

36 PSI

32 PSI

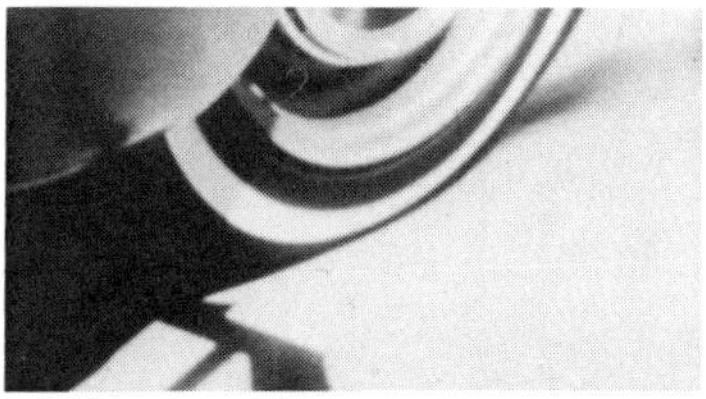

28 PSI

24 PSI

20 PSI

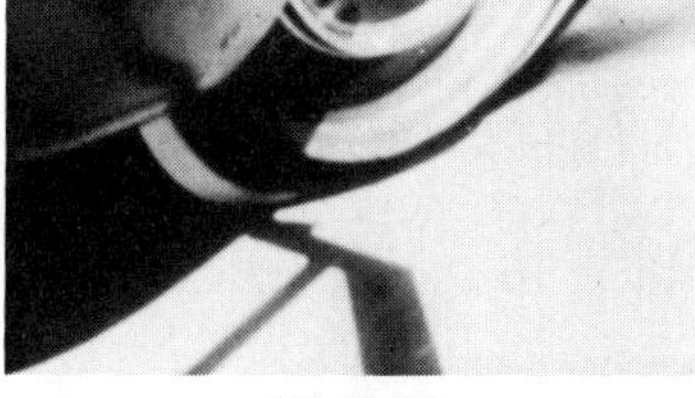

16 PSI

Figure 4.9. These photographs show how underinflation causes roll-under in a cornering tire.

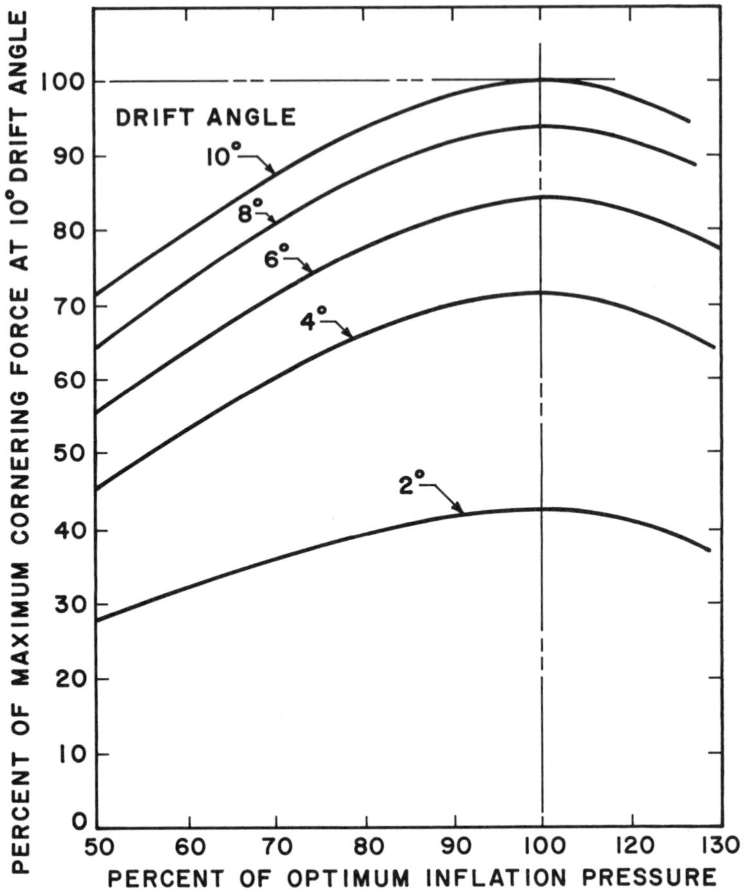

Figure 4.10. Percent of maximum cornering force at various drift angles vs percent of optimum tire inflation pressure (typical tire performance).

psi. Note that the steering angle at 36 and 40 psi are approximately equal. At 32 psi there is a slight increase in steering angle. At 28 psi there is a significant increase in steering angle required to maintain the vehicle in the curve. At 24 psi and less the steering wheel was turned to full lock but the vehicle could not be maintained within the limits of the curve. The reason the vehicle left the curve can be seen in Figure 4.10 which shows there is a typical 18% decrease in available cornering force at 10° drift angle when the tire pressure is lowered 33% (36 to 24 psi). It should be stressed that Figure 4.10 illustrates the performance of *typical* tires but the performance from tire brand to tire brand will vary considerably, some tires being more sensitive than others to tire pressure, particularly at the higher drift angles when the tire is approaching the loss of adhesion.

Looking back at Figure 4.9 it is easy to understand why a tire is unable to develop full cornering force when the tread is rolled under, producing a tire footprint which largely consists of sidewall! The photographs in Figure 4.9 were of the roll-under of the front outside tire on a compact car. Other high speed movies taken of a standard four door sedan in maximum effort cornering with the outside front tire inflated to 24 psi have shown the tire rolled under similar to the 16 psi photograph in Figure 4.9. Figure 4.11 shows the cross section of a typical 24 psi tire in a high speed corner on a standard passenger car. Note that only the tip of the bead is sealing in the air and preventing the tire from deflating suddenly.

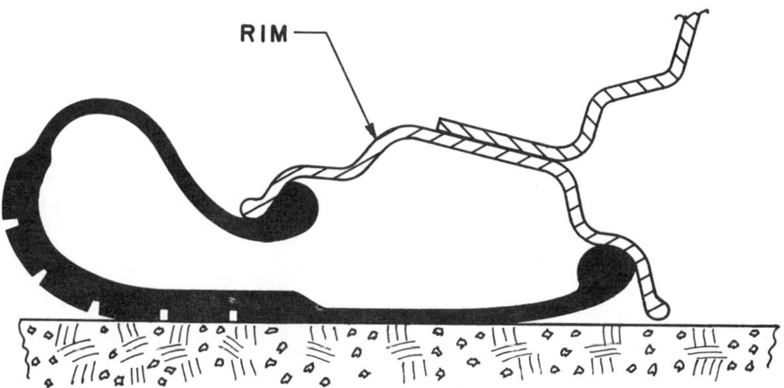

Figure 4.11. This is a cross section of a tire and rim in a high-speed cornering maneuver with 24 psi inflation pressure.

Tubeless tires can lose a substantial amount of air or suddenly "go flat" completely under these conditions.

It has been shown with high speed movies that at 36 psi the standard sedan's bias ply or bias ply belted tires will remain relatively undistorted with almost a complete tread footprint even under "spinout" conditions where complete loss of control occurs. The same is true with steel belted radial ply tires with only 32 psi.

Understeer, Neutral Steer, and Oversteer

One point that is virtually unknown to the average motorist is that by increasing the tire inflation pressure and, thus, the cornering force, it is possible to "tailor" the handling characteristics of most vehicles.

First, we must determine the meaning and significance of "understeer, neutral steer, and oversteer." Figure 4.12 shows vehicles exhibiting these three characteristics as they go through a left turn. All vehicles have developed a vehicle drift angle to produce a cornering force on the rear tires. In the case of the understeer vehicle the center of gravity is located forward of the vehicle's center ($0.4l$), so the front tires have to develop more cornering force than the rear tires. To do this it is necessary to increase the drift angle on the front tires by steering into the curve, because with greater weight in front the vehicle's front end will "push off" the curve unless the front cornering force is increased. This is what happens with equal tire pressures front and rear on the majority of all front engine U.S. passenger vehicles.

If the vehicle is well designed it can be a neutral steer vehicle so that essentially a small or negligible steering angle is required once the vehicle drift angle has been developed. A neutral steer vehicle is highly desirable and the safest handling vehicle of all since there is always adequate steering angle in reserve to turn the vehicle into or out of the curve in an

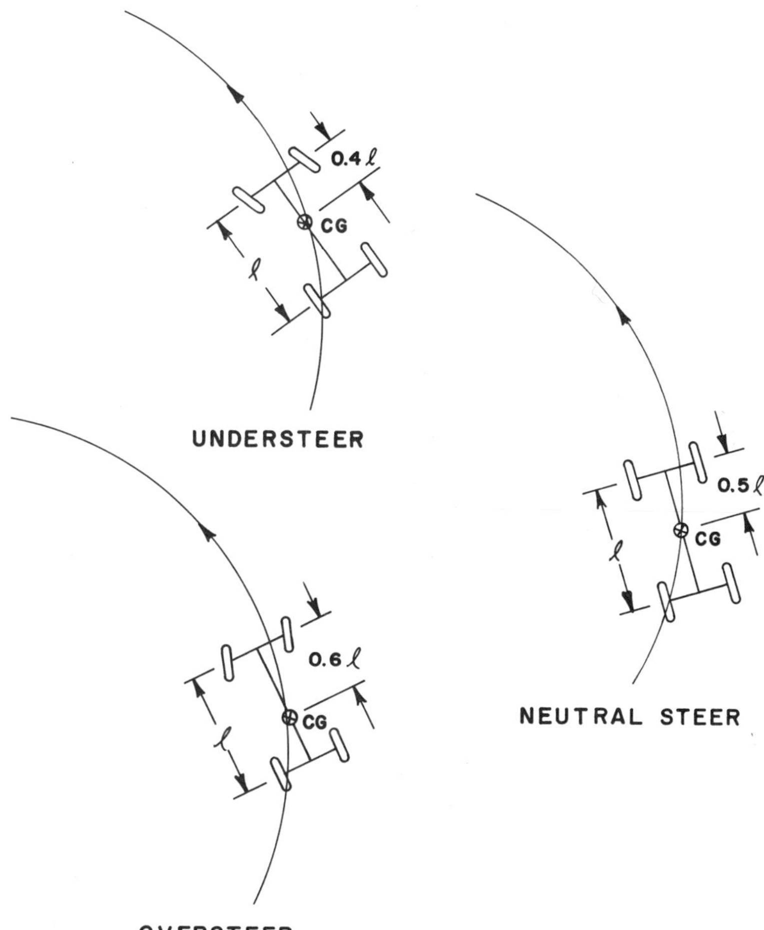

Figure 4.12. Note the front wheel positions and location of center of gravity in these diagrams of understeer, oversteer, and neutral steer.

emergency. In contrast, a heavily understeer vehicle penetrating a curve close to the limits of adhesion may not have sufficient steering angle in reserve to tighten the radius of curvature in an emergency. The understeer vehicle is an easier vehicle to drive for a conservative driver of less than average skill because it tends to keep moving straight ahead in normal straight-away driving. Because of the vehicle's responsive steering, the neutral steer vehicle is much preferred by the better-than-average driver who is prone to drive at the speed limit or the limiting speed for conditions.

The oversteer vehicle with the weight behind the vehicle's center (0.6*l*) requires steering out of the turn because the rear tires must develop more drift angle than the front tires so that they can develop the extra required cornering force. An oversteer vehicle is, by far, the most difficult vehicle to handle. Some of the rear engine oversteer vehicles have been known to display some treacherous spin-out and loss-of-control characteristics when subjected to adverse road conditions or during emergency avoidance maneuvers. A better-than-average driver can learn to anticipate and "lead" the loss of control and will probably experience no serious difficulties, but this type of vehicle handling is not recommended for the unskilled driver or the driver with slow reflexes who wishes to drive fast. As emergency vehicle drivers you may be driving modular design ambulances, which are basically heavy oversteer vehicles because of the extra load on the rear wheels. With equal tire pressures front and rear these vehicles are definitely going to be *oversteer.* But as mentioned previously, it is possible to use the tire pressure effect on cornering force to change a vehicle's handling characteristics. By lowering the tire inflation pressure below optimum inflation pressure the cornering force will be reduced for a given vehicle drift angle to correct oversteer. By "tailoring" the pressure of the front or rear tires up or down, it is possible to obtain the required amount of cornering force for a given vehicle drift angle to correct for most unfavorable weight distributions.

The author experimented with one of the modular ambulance designs that is heavily oversteer when using belted bias ply tires inflated to 60 psi in the front and rear. The maximum cornering force on the truck tires on the modular ambulance occurs at a higher inflation pressure than the 36 psi generally accepted as optimum for a passenger vehicle. By reducing the relatively lightly loaded front tires to 40 psi it was possible to change the modular ambulance to a completely neutral steer vehicle that handled like a sports car. Student drivers, after driving this vehicle with correctly "tuned" tire inflation pressures were amazed at the rapid, responsive steering and excellent handling.

An experienced professional driver can tell immediately whether a vehicle is oversteer, neutral steer, or oversteer but there is one certain way for the average driver to tell. If there is a traffic circle or a long continuous radius curve available for vehicle testing during off hours, start on the curve at 15-20 mph and note the steering wheel position. Increase speed by 5 mph and note the wheel position again. Keep increasing in 5 mph increments until the vehicle's tires are beginning to protest. If, as you speed up, you must turn the steering wheel further and further *into* the curve, then the vehicle is *understeer. If,* as you speed up, you must turn the steering wheel *out* of the curve, then the vehicle is *oversteer.* A neutral steer vehicle will maintain approximately the same steering angle regardless of speed, except in a few cases where slight understeer up to a certain speed and then a slight or even heavy oversteer occurs as the limit of adhesion is approached. This latter tendency normally results from the increased thrust on the rear wheels that is required to maintain the higher cornering speeds. The increased thrust causes a reduction in the effective cornering force on the rear wheels for a given drift angle. This in turn requires steering out of the turn to reduce the drift angle on the front tires. Sudden removal of the driver's foot from the accelerator will cause an immediate recovery of the full cornering force on the rear tires with some violent and unexpected changes in the drift angle of the vehicle (See Chapter 2).

An understeer passenger vehicle, with a front mounted engine, can normally be "tuned" to a neutral steer by using 3 to 5 psi more pressure in the front tires, i.e., 36 psi-front, 33 to 30 psi in the rear. With a full load of passengers and trunk load of baggage the center of gravity would move rearward, thus requiring the rear tire inflation pressures to be raised upward to 36 psi to equalize front and rear tire pressures in order to maintain a neutral steer vehicle.

After you have "tuned" your emergency vehicle for best handling *check your tire pressures daily! Don't depend on anyone else to do it!* In a limit of adhesion cornering maneuver your life can depend on having the proper tire inflation pressure. That corner you can drive through with ease at an entry speed of 38-40 mph with proper tire pressures may be completely unmanageable with incorrect tire pressures.

There is a real danger in becoming overconfident in the handling of your modular ambulance after the tire pressures are correctly adjusted. Don't try to "dirt track" the vehicle through the corners with too much power. As previously mentioned, the two inside wheels can come off the ground if you suddenly release the accelerator under a high drift angle situation. Remember, if you put the vehicle up on the two outside wheels, steer immediately to the *outside* of the turn. If done rapidly enough, this will normally set the vehicle back on all 4 wheels. Otherwise you will turn the vehicle over on its side.

It was mentioned that low tire inflation pressures can waste gasoline, an important factor in these days of high fuel cost. A typical passenger car tire shows a 29% increase in rolling resistance when the inflation pressure is lowered from 36 psi to 24 psi. At 55 mph, if a passenger vehicle normally receives 13½-16 miles per gallon with 36 psi tire inflation pressure, the 24 psi inflation pressure can cause a loss of 1½ to 2 miles per gallon at that speed. This loss coupled with the ability to obtain 40-45,000 miles at 36 psi on a set of tires instead of 20-25,000 miles makes a strong economic point for higher tire inflation pressures.

Tire Hydroplaning

Researchers who have been active in highway safety over the last decade or more have been derelict in their duty in educating the general public about tire hydroplaning. It is a ridiculous situation that such a common cause of accidents on rain soaked highways should be such an unknown hazard to vast numbers of motorists.

NASA first started investigating tire hydroplaning when aircraft landing in standing water on the runways experienced loss of control and "ground looped" as they left the runway surface. In controlled tests NASA discovered that tires would ride up on a film of water at high speed and separate from contact with the runway surface. When the tire footprint rides up on the water film the tire slows down and finally stops revolving causing all steering or braking control to disappear. When this occurs it feels as though the tires are sliding on a greased glass surface and turning the steering wheel in any direction does not change the attitude of the vehicle. If this happens on a curve the vehicle leaves the curve in a straight line. On the straightaway the front end can rotate around and put the vehicle in a violent spin-out into the path of an on-coming vehicle. NASA made an excellent movie (Product 588T-Tire Hydroplaning) that illustrates clearly what starts hydroplaning. The movie shows both passenger vehicle and large aircraft tires as they hydroplane, as well as showing the effect on both types of vehicles when hydroplaning starts. As the NASA films explain, tire hydroplaning can be compared to a water skier being pulled behind a boat. Moving slowly the skier drags through the water. As the speed of the boat increases the water skis start to ride up on to the surface of the water and eventually the skis are skimming across the surface of the water. So it is with the tires. At low speeds they can push the layer of water aside and contact the road surface. As the speed increases there just isn't enough time for the water to flow out from under the tire footprint so the tire rides up on the water that is still left under the footprint.

Figure 4.13 illustrates the interaction between a tire and the water on the surface of the road. In this illustration the viewer is looking up through a glass plate covered with water and the

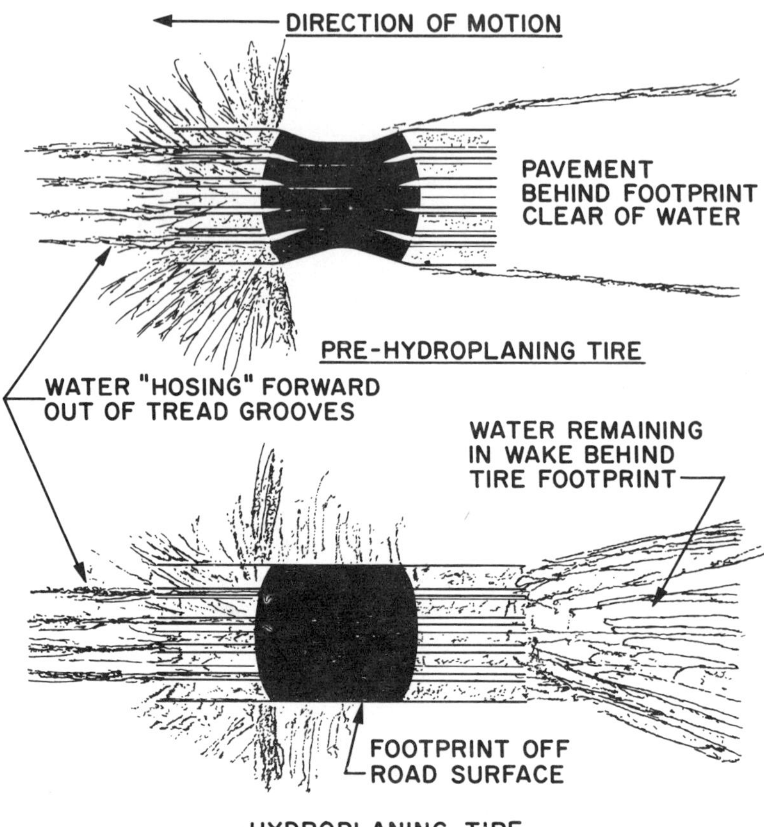

Figure 4.13. Shown here are the kinematics of a hydroplaning tire.

tire is moving from right to left. In the pre-hydroplaning stage the tirc is displacing the water and making contact with the road surface. The water is finding the easiest and shortest path to escape from the "squeeze" between the tire and the road surface. It squirts out in a forward direction through the tread grooves and in a 180° arc in a general spray in front of the tire. Behind the tire the pavement is essentially clear of water and the rear wheels of the vehicle are riding in little or no water.

As the tire begins to hydroplane the footprint clears the road surface and there is no traction between the tire and the road surface. The water is still trying to escape by the easiest and shortest path from under the footprint but there is insufficient time for it to flow out and escape from the "Squeeze". There is still an appreciable amount of water remaining on the road surface behind the tire since the hydroplaning tire could not displace all of it.

A number of factors can affect the speed at which hydroplaning can start. Tire pressure is an important factor and its effect on the starting speed for hydroplaning is shown approximately by the following formula

$$V = 10 \quad \sqrt{\text{Tire Pressure} - \text{psi}}$$

where

$$V = \text{Velocity (mph)}$$

Therefore with 25 psi in the tires hydroplaning will start at

$$V = 10 \quad \sqrt{25} = 10\ (5) = 50 \text{ mph}$$

at 36 psi,

$$V = 10 \quad \sqrt{36} = 10(6) = 60 \text{ mph.}$$

The higher tire pressure helps to prevent the tread grooves from closing up thus allowing some space for the water to move in to. The tread grooves being open have a strong influence on the minimum speed for the start of hydroplaning. Badly worn tires with shallow grooves will hydroplane at a significantly lower speed than new tires with deep grooves. Under identical conditions, steel belted radials with their high lateral stiffness resist closing of the grooves in the footprint area and as a result have a higher minimum speed for the start of hydroplaning than conventional bias ply tires.

Depth of water obviously has a significant effect but hydroplaning can start in water only an ⅛ of an inch deep or shallower. Deep standing puddles on the road can start hydroplaning at much lower speeds. There is always a danger after a heavy rain that as the road surface starts to dry off the motorists will resume their previous speed. Normally there are depressions in most old road surfaces that can trap and hold standing water. Impact with these standing puddles at highway speeds can initiate hydroplaning and consequent loss of control and a spin-out.

In heavy rains or in the period immediately after a heavy rain slow down below your minimum possible hydroplaning speed, otherwise your first experience with hydroplaning may be your last!

There's an old war adage, "It's the one you don't see that kills you."

5 EXPECT THE UNEXPECTED

On an emergency run there is no guarantee that all traffic will magically melt and flow to one side in response to your warning signal and flasher lights. Remember there are "Nervous Nellies", psychotics, drunks, mentally and emotionally disturbed people, drivers on drugs and medications, and confused, elderly people operating motor vehicles. One accident study in a large city showed on the basis of a cursory psychoanalysis of 155 accident-involved drivers that one out of six was either deeply emotionally disturbed or should have been under the care of a psychiatrist. One out of twenty should have been committed to a mental institution. *Remember this* if you are tempted to trust another driver to take the correct driving action. No one knows what some drivers are likely to do when an emergency vehicle overtakes them since they are not certain themselves. One common occurrence, reported by experienced emergency drivers, is that drivers may slam on the brakes and stop in the middle of the street when they become terrified by the flashing lights and the screaming siren. So look out! Expect the unexpected!

Don't be fooled into believing that everyone can hear your siren or yelper. Some people driving air conditioned vehicles while listening to their radios are completely oblivious to street sounds. Also, there are elderly drivers with impaired hearing who, if their vehicles' windows are closed, cannot hear your siren. These are only two examples of dozens of special cases where it is impossible for the driver to hear your warning signal. Even if they do hear you, they may turn in front of you just as you start to pass. By carefully watching the vehicles ahead you may be able to determine whether the drivers have heard your warning signal, since they may be taking some form of evasive action. However, you cannot be sure of what kind of evasive action it might be. Don't trust the average driver to perform the proper evasive action!

A very skilled and experienced EMS driver was surprised at an intersection as he approached a red light on a Code 3 run. Pulling to the left of a vehicle waiting at the light, he braked his ambulance to almost a complete stop. He proceeded to turn right, in front of the stopped vehicle, with his warning signal blaring and his flasher lights on. The light changed just as he turned right and the "dear little old gray-haired lady," driving the stopped vehicle, accelerated and rammed into the side of his ambulance. "I didn't hear it or see it" was her answer. Obviously there was no way the EMS driver could avoid this accident or predict what the other driver was going to do. In any emergency driving some chances must be taken, but it is necessary to minimize these chances as much as humanly possible within the limitations of providing an efficient emergency driving service.

There is an ever present danger in answering emergency calls in shopping areas where the streets are lined with plate glass windows at the intersections. If two emergency vehicles approach the same intersection simultaneously at a right angle to each other, it is quite possible that the reflection of one vehicle's flasher lights will camouflage the other's. This resulting confusion has resulted in a number of serious intersection accidents. Be alert at the intersections and don't cling to the idea that your emergency warning system will always provide you with a shield of complete protection. Murphy's Law, "If it can be done wrong it will be," still applies to this part of emergency driving, and the next driver you encounter may be just the one to do it wrong!

Don't feel secure in having the green light in going through an intersection. There are careless drivers and drunken drivers that are going to run through those red lights. In the Alcohol Safety Action program surveys that have been conducted around the U.S. it is not unusual to find that between the hours of 7 p.m. and 2 a.m. on Friday and Saturdays, 12 to 20% of the drivers are intoxicated above the legal limit of .10% blood-alcohol. These drunks can come "cannon-balling" through a red light without slowing down or looking right or left.

Keep your eyes alert in passing buses discharging passengers. Watch under the front of the bus for feet walking out into the traffic. Sometimes just the shadow of the feet will be all that can be seen, but it can alert a careful driver.

Children running out between parked cars, jaywalking pedestrians, children riding bikes randomly all over the street, all constitute real threats to the life of the careless person and can be a real threat to the emergency driver who is taking evasive action to avoid hitting them.

Often, when driving faster than legal speeds, the emergency driver can surprise the average driver on the road. Some drivers, because they lack depth perception and judgement, are unable to estimate the closing speed of an oncoming vehicle. If they are accustomed to pulling out in front of an oncoming vehicle that is traveling 30 mph when it is a certain distance away, then they may pull out in front of an emergency vehicle traveling at 60 mph when it is the same distance away.

When passing vehicles, watch their front tires and their position with respect to the paint stripe between lanes. If the front tire is suddenly moving closer to the paint stripe the driver is probably getting ready to change lanes and pull out into your path. Watching the front tire can be done in the corner of your visual field without taking your main attention from the road ahead. Watch those tires closely and avoid a side swiping accident.

All of the above mentioned hazards are merely representative examples of the unlimited number of calamities that can befall an emergency driver. It is impossible to describe *every* danger that might be encountered on an emergency run. The best that can be done is to provide each emergency driver with the foresight to recognize a dangerous situation and the ability to overcome it. In other words, always *expect the unexpected.*

Taking the Escape Route

Although you may be the most astute driver in the world, there may come the time in your emergency driving when your vehicle leaves the road surface because you have lost control or you have steered it off the road to avoid a collision. Many drivers feel that "all is lost" if they leave the road. Far from it! When it is impossible to stop in time to avoid an accident it *may be* far more desirable to leave the road before impacting the obstacle or vehicle in the road ahead. The *may be* depends upon the presence or absence of roadside obstacles, the type of roadside obstacles, and the terrain on the side of the road. This will require split second judgment and quick evasive action. Your life and the lives of your passengers depend upon your correct choice and quick action.

First, is the ground to the side of the road relatively level and clear of deep bar ditches or open drainage ditches running under the road? Yes? So far, so good because a wide, shallow bar ditch running parallel to the road can be taken without rolling over. But if the ditch has steep banks, or is a transverse ditch, i.e., it runs at a 90° angle to the road, stay on the road because impact of your vehicle with the far side of the ditch will stop you very suddenly! Are there any utility poles of 5 inches or larger in diameter, large trees, or large traffic sign support posts that you will hit? These obstacles have a nasty tendency to cut through your vehicle like a dull knife. It may be safer to stay on the road and impact the stopped vehicle ahead. The decision is yours to make and you don't have much time!

Some obstacles can be hit without serious danger. Bushes and shrubbery hit while traveling straight will slow down the vehicle with minimal damage. "Breakaway" sign supports and breakaway aluminum street light supports mounted on a concrete base approximately at the ground level can be struck without serious damage to the vehicle or its occupants. At least they will be considerably "softer" than a motionless vehicle in the road ahead. Be certain that the base of the street light support does not come up high enough to catch your front bumper, frame, or front suspension system. That concrete base is very solid and will cause a disastrously short stop of your vehicle.

You will find it helpful as you drive at normal speeds along roads in your operational zone to study the sides of the road and see where you can find safe escape routes. Make decisions about marginally safe escape routes. It is far better to make the important decisions when you have ample time. If necessary, when you are off duty, come back and walk over some of the questionable areas for a closer examination. A detailed study will permit you to answer some of the following questions:

1. Would it be safe to angle out through that bar ditch?
2. Could I safely crash through that hedge or fence line?
3. Would it be safe after a rain to drive at speed through the grassy area or is the mud too soft?
4. What is the actual height of the concrete base on the street light?

It may seem foolish and a waste of time to do this, but this kind of knowledge accumulated ahead of time may save your life or avoid serious injury some day. Successful and experienced road racing drivers will "walk out" and inspect on foot all curves and critical maneuvering areas of a new course so that they can find the safe escape routes if they need them during the actual race. Their decisions have been made ahead of time—so should yours, if at all possible.

After leaving the road surface use your brakes as heavily as possible without losing control. If you are on a flat, level field there is no necessity for a panic stop, but if there could be hidden ditches or stumps get your vehicle stopped as rapidly as possible without losing control.

If you have entered into a corner too fast and are unable to maintain a safe drift angle, you will be forced to "straighten out the curve" and leave the road surface. If you know you aren't going to be able to stay on the road surface, straighten out your front wheels. Do not hit the soft ground or grass with your front wheels in a high drift angle. High speed movies of tires taken during a vehicle spin-out show that the tire stops rotating when the tire drift angle exceeds 25-30°. This is a little known fact but one that can be deadly if your front tires hit soft ground, grass or weeds, loose gravel and rock while in a high drift angle. When the tire stops rotating it acts as a bulldozer blade and starts a build-up of material ahead of the tire (see Figure 5.1). When the drag of the material ahead of the tire becomes excessive, the tire stops moving sideways but the vehicle doesn't, causing the vehicle to overturn and somersault from corner to corner. In investigating overturning accidents involving vehicles which have left the road, it is normally possible to find a long wide wheel track with a pile of material at its end where the vehicle started rolling over. If the driver had straightened his front wheels to keep the front wheels turning, there would have been no chance for a build-up of material against the side of the tire and the overturning of the vehicle would have been avoided.

There may be a time when there is no clear escape route to avoid a collision. You must then select the "softest spot". Hit-

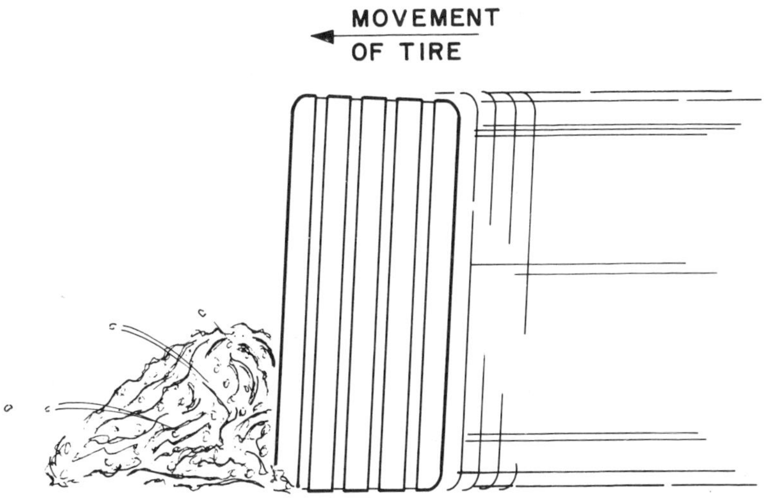

Figure 5.1. The buildup of material in front of a nonrotating tire in a high vehicle angle can cause the vehicle to overturn.

ting the "soft spot" will mean impacting the obstruction that will slow your vehicle down the least amount, that is, striking whatever object that will produce the lowest velocity change. Vehicles striking each other follow approximately the laws of momentum. The momentum of a vehicle is proportional to mv, where m = mass or weight, and v = velocity. The sum of the momentum of the two vehicles before, after, and during impact is the same. This is only approximately true since there is energy or momentum absorbed by deformation of the vehicles striking one another. However, the law of momentum gives us a good approximation of the maximum probable velocity change.

Figure 5.2 illustrates the law of momentum applied to four different cases: Case A—vehicles traveling in the same direction at different speeds; Case B—one vehicle stopped and being struck by a moving vehicle; Case C—vehicles traveling in opposite directions at different speeds: Case D—vehicles

Continued on page 88

Case A—Two vehicles traveling in the same direction at different speeds.

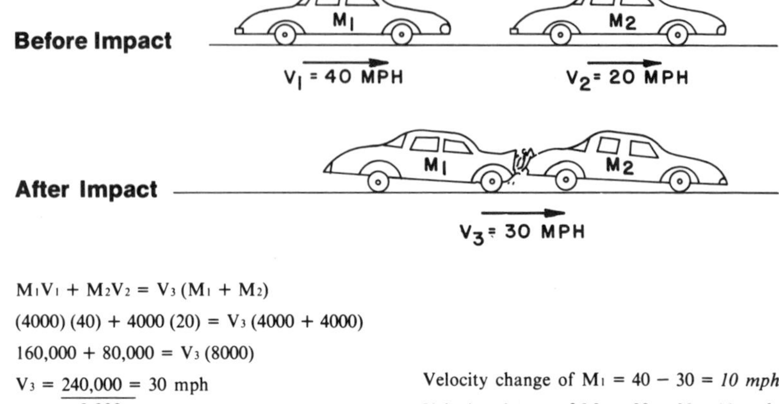

$M_1V_1 + M_2V_2 = V_3(M_1 + M_2)$

$(4000)(40) + 4000(20) = V_3(4000 + 4000)$

$160{,}000 + 80{,}000 = V_3(8000)$

$V_3 = \frac{240{,}000}{8{,}000} = 30$ mph

Velocity change of $M_1 = 40 - 30 =$ *10 mph*

Velocity change of $M_2 = 30 - 20 =$ *10 mph*

Case B—A stopped vehicle being struck by a moving vehicle.

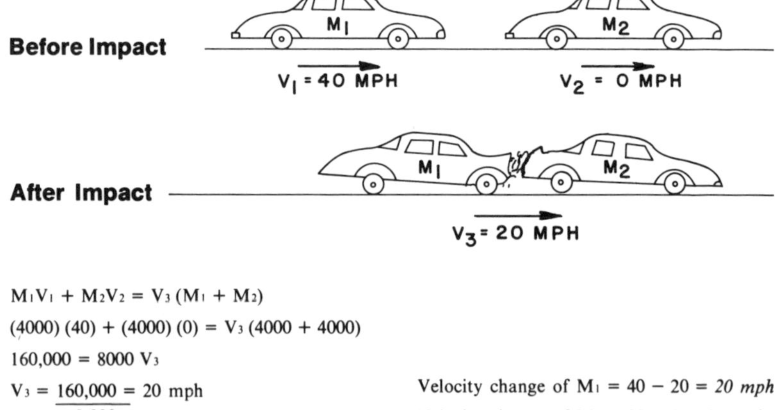

$M_1V_1 + M_2V_2 = V_3(M_1 + M_2)$

$(4000)(40) + (4000)(0) = V_3(4000 + 4000)$

$160{,}000 = 8000\,V_3$

$V_3 = \frac{160{,}000}{8{,}000} = 20$ mph

Velocity change of $M_1 = 40 - 20 =$ *20 mph*

Velocity change of $M_2 = 20 - 0 =$ *20 mph*

Figure 5.2. Cases A, B, C, *and* D *show how speed and direction affect a collision between two vehicles.**

Case C—Two vehicles traveling in opposite directions at different speeds.

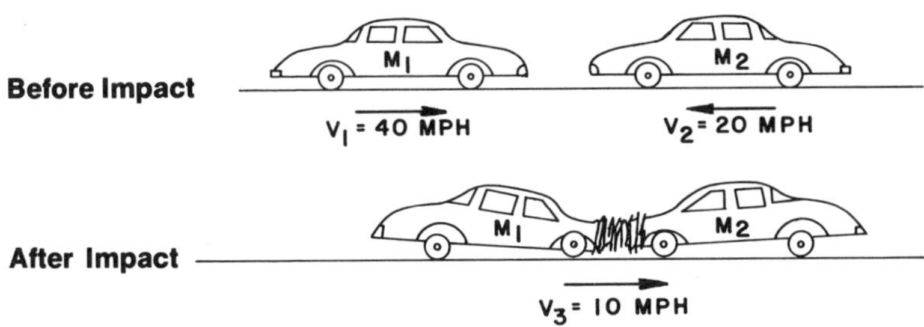

$M_1V_1 + M_2V_2 = V_3(M_1 + M_2)$

Since vehicles are moving in opposite directions, V_2 is a negative value.

$(4000)(40) + (4000)(-20) = V_3(4000 + 4000)$

$160{,}000 - 80{,}000 = 8000\,V_3$

$V_3 = \frac{80{,}000}{8{,}000} = 10$ mph

Velocity change of $M_1 = (40 - 10) =$ *30 mph*

Velocity change of $M_2 = -20 - 10 =$ *⁻30 mph*

Case D—Two vehicles traveling in opposite directions at the same speed.

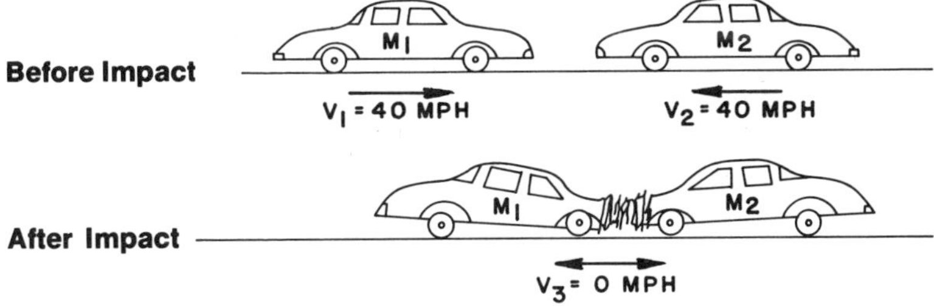

$M_1V_1 = M_2V_2 = V_3(M_1 + M_2)$

Since vehicles are moving in opposite directions, V_2 is a negative value.

$(4000)(40) + (4000)(-40) = V_3(4000 + 4000)$

$160{,}000 - 160{,}000 = 8000V_3$

$V_3 = \frac{0}{8000} = 0$ mph

Velocity change of $M_1 = 40 - 0 =$ *40 mph*

Velocity change of $M_2 = -40 - (-0) =$ *40 mph*

**Assume the weight of the emergency vehicle and the passenger vehicle is 4000 lbs in each case.*

traveling in opposite directions at the same speed. There is an increasing level of velocity change for the emergency vehicle from Case A to Case D, ranging from a low of 10 mph for Case A to 40 mph for Case D.

When driving a modular ambulance, remember that you are maneuvering about 8000 lbs of equipment through the streets and highways at high speeds. The advantage of this extra weight in a collision with a 4000-lb passenger vehicle can be seen in Case D of Figure 5.2. In a head-on collision with both vehicles traveling at 40 mph, the modular ambulance will experience a velocity change of only 27 mph instead of the 40 mph velocity change in the case of the 4000-lb passenger vehicle.

Suppose the road ahead is blocked suddenly by a multiple car accident or a jack-knifed semi-trailer. What is the safest way to leave the road surface if it is impossible to brake to a complete stop? Referring to Figure 5.3, in this hypothetical case, the emergency vehicle driver starts braking from 60 mph, 374 ft from the jack-knifed semi-trailer. The road surface is slick, wet Tarvia with a coefficient of friction of 0.2 ($\mu = 0.2$) We can use Equation (3.1) from Chapter 3 to calculate the stopping distance required.

$$S = V^2/2\mu g$$

where

S = Stopping distance (ft)
V = Velocity (ft/sec)
μ = Coefficient of friction
g = Acceleration of gravity, 32.16 ft/sec^2

Referring to Figure 5.3:

V = 60 mph = 88 ft/sec
μ = 0.2

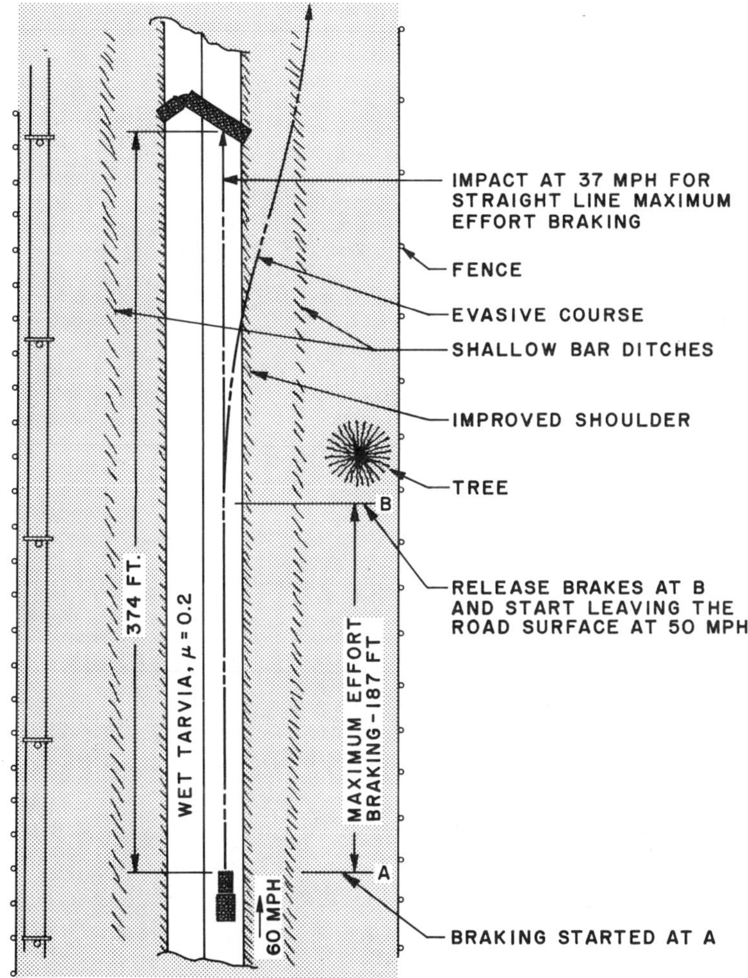

Figure 5.3. When leaving the road surface becomes necessary, fast, accurate judgement can mean the difference between a controlled spinout and an end-over-end disaster.

Substituting in Equation (3.1)

$$S = (88)^2/2(0.2)(32.16) = 602 \text{ ft}$$

Because the jack-knifed semi-trailer is only 374 ft away it will be necessary to leave the road surface to avoid a collision.

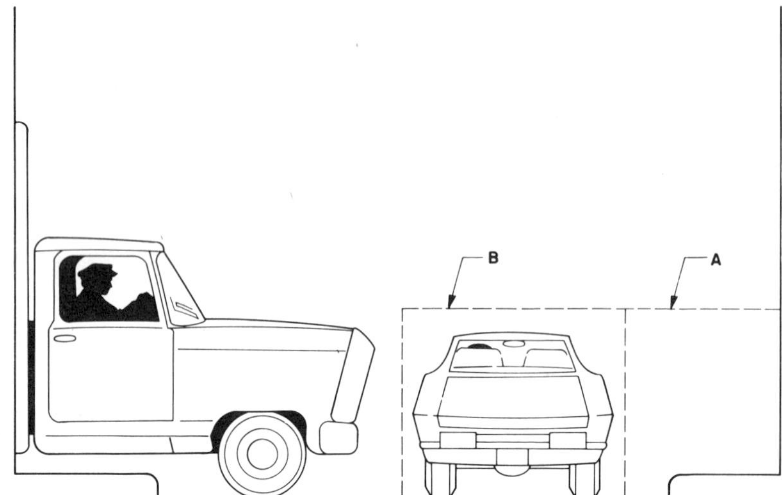

Figure 5.4. Which of these escape routes is the best to take? It depends on the circumstances.

First, brake as heavily as possible without locking up a wheel and starting a skid. Brake down to point B, then release the brakes and leave the road surface with careful, smooth steering to prevent loss of control on the slick pavement. During the 2.3 seconds of braking before leaving the road, the driver should have checked for escape routes to the left and right of the obstacle in the road ahead. In Figure 5.3 it can be seen that there is a line of utility poles on the left hand side. Both sides of the road have shallow bar ditches, so the right side is safest. By angling carefully through the shallow bar ditch beyond the tree on the right side, the vehicle can be braked to a stop carefully while maintaining complete control. Quick thinking, careful evasive action, and skillful driving can enable one to avoid most hazardous situations.

Figure 5.4 illustrates a hypothetical accident situation in which you are approaching an intersection, and your overtaking speed is such that you can pass the vehicle in your lane after passing the intersection. A truck pulls out into the intersection and completely blocks the left lane, and the frightened driver of the car ahead makes a panic stop blocking the right lane. You cannot stop in time. Which escape area should you take, "A" or "B"? If the right hand brick wall is a series of store fronts then take the "B" area. The driver has a headrest so will probably not suffer whiplash or serious injury. If someone steps out of a door when you take the "A" area it would be sudden death for him. Your time to make the most humane and just choice to minimize injury or loss of life is short.

Hitting the heavy tractor of the semi-trailer would not injure the truck driver but it would stop your emergency vehicle very suddenly and possibly kill or seriously injure you and your passengers. These alternatives have to be weighed instantly and the best choice made without hesitation. Such is the nature of emergency driving.

Ultimately, it is the driver's actions which determine the success or failure of an emergency run.

6 YOU, THE DRIVER

The success or failure of an emergency run ultimately depends upon the driver's performance. Just as the vehicle must be kept in top operating condition, it is necessary for you, as an emergency driver, to maintain yourself in top condition so that you can perform all the necessary driver functions as rapidly and efficiently as humanly possible.

Driver's Position

First, let us review the recommended position of the driver's body, hands, and feet for emergency driving. The "name of the game" in emergency driving is to get the hands, feet, and body into the correct position as soon as possible with the least amount of hesitation or delay and with the minimum number of errors.

The Body

The body should be directly behind the steering wheel in an upright position. It should not be slumped over against the door or leaning back in a semi-reclining position. On a high-speed run you will find that by sitting upright and leaning slightly forward at the waist you will be instantly ready for any corrective driving action that may be required. Your muscles should be tensed like a sprinter on his starting blocks so that you are ready to trigger whatever immediate physical movement is needed.

The Hands

The author recommends the hand position shown in Figure 6.1A, the ten minutes after ten (10:10) position for rapid and accurate corrective steering. This hand position on the steering wheel works well with the upright body position recommended above. Instant right or left, high speed avoidance steering can be accomplished without moving the hands on the steering wheel rim. This is important in rapid lane changes or in avoiding a pedestrian or bicyclist. Under these conditions there is insufficient time to change hand position on the wheel since the corrective steering needs to be an almost instantaneous reflex action by the driver. Many driving instructors recommend a 10:20 (20 minutes after 10) hand position. This is fine for all-day driving since it puts the arms in a comfortable, less tiring position, but it limits the degree of instantaneous right turn steering that can be done before changing hand positions on the steering wheel. If the right hand remains on the steering wheel it moves into an awkward position under the left arm.

Figure 6.1B illustrates the movement of the left hand to permit more steering in a sharp turn to the right. If "full lock steering" is required the right hand moves counterclockwise about 120° (a third of the distance around the wheel) to regrasp the steering wheel so more steering can be introduced into the front wheels. In a sharp turn to the left the hand movements are reversed with the right hand first moving about 120° clockwise and then the left hand moving clockwise 120°

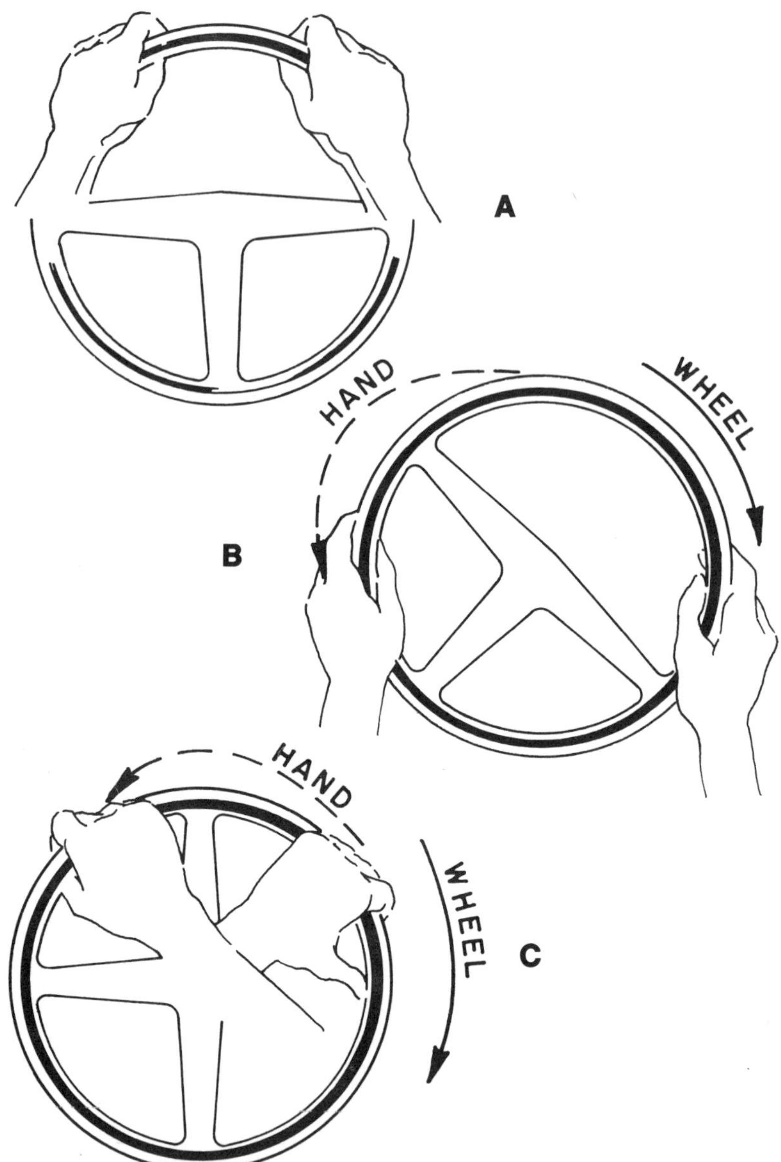

Figure 6.1. Shown here are the recommended hand positions for emergency driving. A *shows the 10:10 hand placement. The correct left hand movement to permit more steering in a sharp right turn is illustrated in* B. *The crossing of the right hand over the left in a sharp right turn, as shown in* C, *is awkward and slow.*

on the wheel to introduce added steering if needed. The recommended steering is a step-by-step progression of the hands around the steering wheel *without* crossing the hands over one another as shown in Figure 6.1C. Crossing hands is a mistake because they become locked over one another and thus inhibit the movement of the hand still on the wheel that is trying to increase or decrease the steering. There is a "built-in delay" in changing the steering if the hands have to be separated to turn the wheel further. A sportscar racing driver accustomed to high speed 90° corners, would never consider getting his hands into this awkward position where there would be a possible slowing of his corrective steering and a reduction in the *precision* of his steering.

The Feet

The hands control the direction of the vehicle and the feet control its speed. The seat should be adjusted forward sufficiently to permit the heel of the right foot to rest on the floorboard with the ball of the right foot on the accelerator when the right leg is in a comfortable position. Be certain to have that right heel resting firmly on the floorboard and not "floating" in mid-air. If the right foot is placed with the heel up on the accelerator then it becomes difficult, if not impossible, to accurately maintain a smooth accelerator control on rough roads, jumping curbs, or in emergency avoidance maneuvers.

The left foot is placed firmly on the floorboard to the left of the brake on long runs on open expressways or interstate highways. When the traffic becomes heavier and a quick stop may be required, the author recommends that you place the heel of the left foot on the floorboard in front of the brake pedal with the ball of the left foot held *close to* but *clear* of the brake pedal. Once you become practiced in using your left foot in this manner, you will find that it effectively reduces your reaction time in applying the brakes. It stands to reason that it takes longer to lift the right foot up off the accelerator, move it in a rearward direction, stop the rearward motion, move it to the left and up, then move it forward and contact the brake. Compare this with merely moving the ball of the left foot forward an inch or so before contacting the brake pedal. It is obvious that the "standby-alert" position of the left foot over the brake pedal will add valuable distance in available road for stopping your vehicle. Using the right foot for braking is probably a hold-over from the days of the manual transmission when it was necessary to release the clutch in making a complete stop. The author habitually uses left foot braking in all his every-day driving with an automatic transmission. Upon encountering dense traffic or approaching a corner or a potentially dangerous traffic situation, it is best to hold the left foot just clear of the brake. For comfort, in between the periods of possible emergency braking, the left heel can be left in line with the brake pedal and the left toe rotated counterclockwise to rest the foot on the floorboard. The toe can be lifted and rotated clockwise as the possible need for instant braking approaches. If you haven't used left foot braking in driving with an automatic transmission, "Try it, you'll like it!"

Never rest your left foot on the brake pedal. This has two bad effects: (1) You will probably cause your brake lights to turn on and the following driver will be unable to tell when you *do* put your brakes on. This creates a dangerous traffic hazard. (2) If your foot pressure is sufficient to cause the brakes to drag you will be wasting expensive fuel and will cause the brakes to heat up, thus reducing their capacity to resist "fading" on a heavy braking stop. In addition, the brake drag will rapidly wear away the brake linings, requiring the brakes to be relined in a relatively few miles. "Riding" the brake is inexcusable for a professional emergency driver.

Physical Condition

The emergency driver, whether he is a pursuit vehicle driver, an ambulance driver, or whatever, should regard himself much in the light of an athlete in training. The top racing drivers, the ones who survive the dangerous game the longest, are the ones who keep themselves in top physical condition. They are mindful of the abuse they have taken before they ask their body and mind to perform at peak performance. Peak performance, which is the ability to see, think, and react correctly with a minimum of delay, may be the difference between life and death. To do this the body and mind must be at its maximum level of response. Peak performance cannot be achieved if the body and mind are handicapped by the effects of alcohol, medication, drugs, or fatigue.

Alcohol

There have been many articles and newspaper stories written on the obvious dangers of the intoxicated driver. Fully half the vehicle oriented accidents and fatalities are currently being blamed on the intoxicated driver. A .10% blood-alcohol level, which is calculated by multiplying the weight of the alcohol in the blood by 100 and dividing by the weight of the blood, is the legal level for intoxication in most states. Some states allow as high as .15% and some have lowered the legal limit to .08%. The author believes, as a result of driving tests he has conducted on drinking drivers, that .10% is too lenient since the drivers at .10% perform with an unacceptable level of driving errors. The .15% drivers could be classified as "sloppy drunk."

The level of intoxication of a drinker depends upon the amount of alcohol consumed, the time in which it is consumed, and the body weight of the drinker. Alcohol is changed by the liver to a sugar that the body can burn as energy. The liver reduces the blood-alcohol content by approximately .010% each hour. According to Department of Transportation findings, if the drinker has consumed sufficient alcohol in one hour to raise the blood-alcohol level to the legal intoxication limit (.10%), then it will take 10 hours at .010% per hour for the liver to convert all the alcohol to sugar. If the drinker is at

.20% when he stops drinking he will still be legally intoxicated 10 hours later! Mathematically it looks like this, .20% − (10 x .010%) = .10%. There is *nothing* that will remove the alcohol from the bloodstream but a good liver and time! Black coffee, cold showers, tomato juice, Worcestershire sauce, sleep, etc. simply are old wives' tales and do nothing but give the drinker a false sense of security that he has been "sobered up." The partying drinker who quits drinking at 2 a.m. with a blood alcohol level of .20% and goes to work at 8 a.m. will still be quite drunk with a blood alcohol level of approximately .15%. If the drinker is an emergency driver he will be a menace to himself and all the other drivers he meets on the road the next morning. He is one of the 8 a.m. drunks.

How many drinks does it take to put your blood-alcohol level at .10%? Figure 6.2 shows the resulting blood alcohol level when a given amount of 80 proof alcohol is consumed in one hour on an "empty stomach" with little or no food eaten before drinking. This is a nomograph and it shows the relation between body weight, ounces of 80 proof liquor consumed, and blood-alcohol concentration in the blood. Obviously it takes less 86 or 100 proof liquor to cause the same condition. Also, one bottle of beer is approximately equal to one ounce of 80 proof liquor. By using a straightedge from the body weight and extending it on through the correct ounces of liquor consumed to the blood-alcohol concentration line we can determine the intoxication level. Or, you can line a straightedge up with your weight and .10%, the legal intoxication limit, and read off how many ounces of 80 proof liquor you must consume in an hour to be legally intoxicated. If your consumption occurs over a period of hours, then it is necessary to multiply .010% by the number of hours during which the drinking occurred and subtract that total from the intoxication level that would have resulted from drinking the entire amount of alcohol in one hour. For instance, referring to Figure 6.2 again, take the line running from 150 lbs through 5 ounces of 80 proof liquor to 0.10%. If this drinking occurred in 3 hours

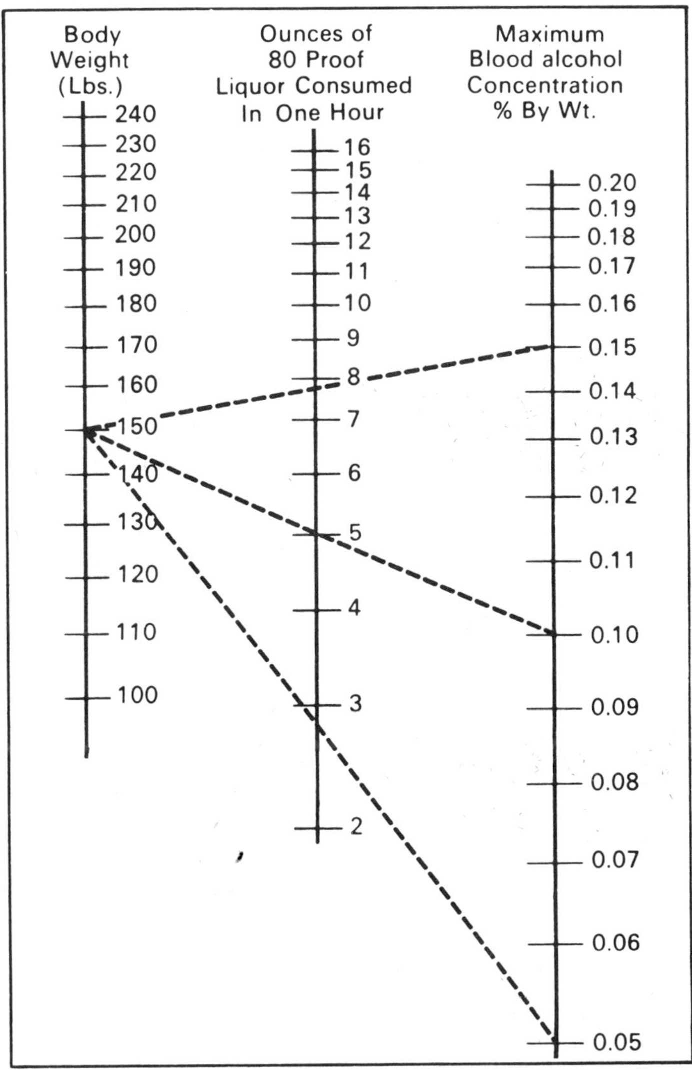

Figure 6.2. Blood alcohol concentration after consuming various amounts of 80 proof liquor in one hour on an empty stomach. (Adapted from a chart by U.S. Department of Health, Education and Welfare.)

the resulting blood-alcohol level would be: .10% − 2 (.010%) = .08%. Since the drinking occurred during an extra 2 hours beyond the one hour period of the chart, the liver has 2 hours to reduce the blood-alcohol.

Professional aircraft pilots and top level racing drivers will not take a drink 24 hours before they require their body and minds to perform at a peak level. It was the author's experience that even 2 drinks the evening before would slow his reaction time and cloud his judgment on the race course the next afternoon, approximately 18 to 20 hours later. There is a definite recovery time needed after the consumption of alcohol for the body and mind to return to its normal state. Those of us who have imbibed too freely and unwisely the night before have been punished by our body with a hangover the next morning. And, it is not until the following day that the body and mind returns to normal, a full 24 hours to 36 hours later.

The "Full Stomach" chart of Figure 6.3 shows that a person with a full stomach can drink about 2 ounces more than a person with an empty stomach and still have the same blood-alcohol level.

Prescription Drugs

If your doctor prescribes drugs for some ailment, you should ask him if there are side effects that could affect your driving. The list of prescription drugs that could have an effect on your driving is too long to cover here, so you should rely on you M.D. to provide this information. Remember to ask him if there are possible side effects and *how long* those side effects might last.

Although no attempt will be made in this book to discuss specific drugs, the classes of drugs that could affect the drivers' performance behind the wheel are listed. One aspect of these drugs is that their effect on a person increases geometrically with the dosage.

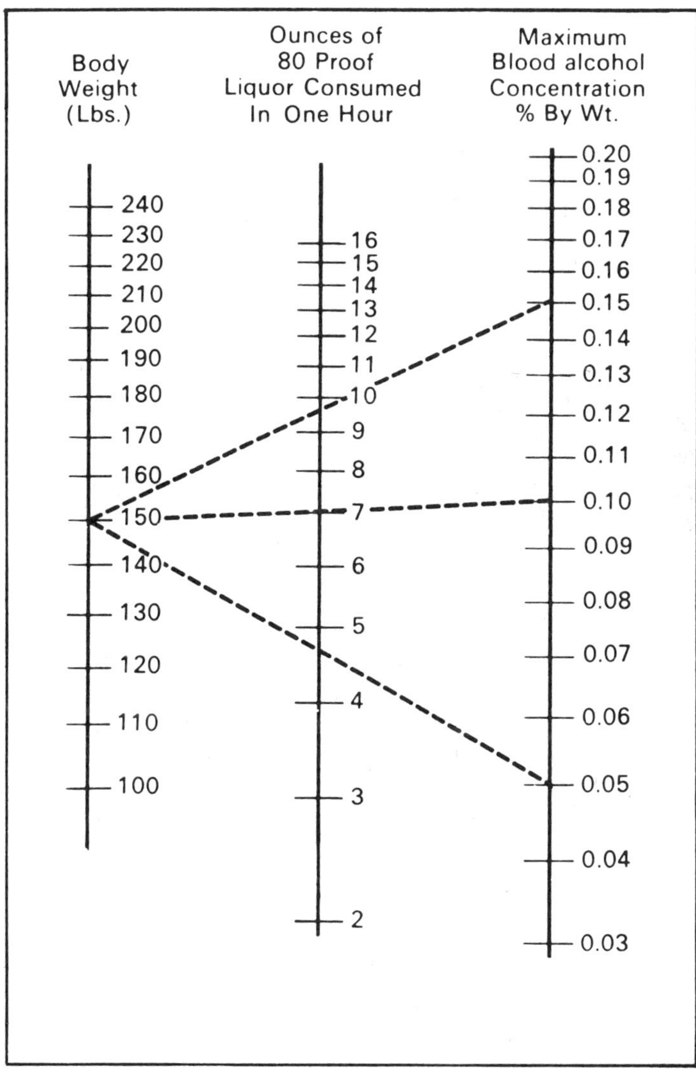

Figure 6.3. Blood alcohol concentration after consuming various amounts of 80 proof liquor in one hour on a full stomach (1-2 hours after an average meal). (Adapted from a chart by Royal Canadian Mounted Police.)

These classes of drugs may affect your driving performance:

1. Tranquilizers—Strong doses of these nerve quieting drugs can have a powerful effect on your driving performance in the form of drowsiness or lack of alertness.
2. Antihistamine (to prevent allergies)—Some of these drugs can cause you to fall asleep at the wheel on a long run.
3. Anti-anxiety/depression—The effect of such drugs is similar to alcohol in that reaction time is slowed and a sense of complacency and relaxation is created.
4. Analgesics (pain killers)—Darvon is one example of this type of drug which, if taken in excessive quantity, can cause a person to be irrational.

Marijuana

The "popularity" of marijuana has been rapidly increasing in recent years, and much has been said in publications and on television about how "harmless" or "harmful" (depending on whose source is cited) marijuana is. There are constant arguments about reducing the penalties for possession of marijuana, even legalizing it completely. For the moment, the clinical and legal pronouncements about marijuana must be left to the fields of medicine and jurisprudence.

However, no matter what else may be said of marijuana, there is the undeniable fact that marijuana use affects the mental state of a person. Whether this effect be euphoria, drowsiness, a slowing sensation of time, abnormal self-confidence, or just silly behavior, the emergency driver, because of his responsibility to himself and the public, cannot be subject to any state of mind which might impair his ability to think clearly and react instantly. Any substance that even slightly restricts an emergency driver's performance should be avoided.

The slowing of the time-speed sense is the most dangerous effect because the driver can be speeding at 120 mph and feel that he is only going 60 mph. Also, a car approaching an intersection at 60 mph may appear to be moving only at 30 mph and the marijuana intoxicated driver may drive out into its path because "it's moving so slowly." The other effects such as exhilaration and increased self-confidence would add to the dangers, causing the driver to charge in at high speed with the feeling, "I can make it OK." He can probably make it to hell on time!

There are studies which indicate that psychotic "flashbacks" can occur as much as two months after a moderate user has stopped smoking marijuana. There is an accumulation in the body of the metabolites (chemical breakdown of the primary drug) of Δ9THC, the psychoactive ingredient in marijuana that produces "the high." It takes up to a week for the body to rid itself of the Δ9THC metabolites that are absorbed from a single cigarette of marijuana. Don't think you can "blow grass" on your day off and then be sure of driving safely because you aren't smoking "on the job." If you smoke just once, every week, your body is never free of the metabolites of Δ9THC.

Fatigue

No one is at their peak physical performance when they are fatigued. The reaction time increases to an unacceptable level for emergency driving situations when the body and mind are tired. *Don't* overexercise before going on duty. Be certain you can get your normal amount of sleep and rest after strenuous activity so that you will report in rested and not physically exhausted. Don't try to watch the late, late movie on TV and then report for an 8 a.m. shift. If you do, you will be unable to respond with peak driving performance if an emergency situation arises. Remember you are jeopardizing your own life as well as the lives of others when you handicap your driving performance by being mentally or physically fatigued.

Vision

Good eyesight is of prime importance in emergency driving. If you require glasses or contact lenses then you probably realize the importance of regular eye examinations by an opthalmologist. If you've never had a thorough eye examination, you owe it to yourself to have one to be certain that your vision is normal and you do not have any eye disease or eye strain caused by imperfect vision. Take care of your eyes and they will take care of you.

Night vision is of utmost importance. At night the driver has an added handicap to his normal reaction time known as perception time. This is the time required to see and recognize the need to stop because of a roadside hazard. This averages about 0.8 second. The majority of the drivers on the road fail to use their high beams when they are able to do so and as a result they are "overdriving" their headlights. That is, by the time they can see a hazard in the road ahead they are already too close for the speed they are driving to avoid an accident. For instance, with low beam headlights it is possible to see a roadside hazard 362 ft down the highway when driving into oncoming headlights. If the driver is traveling at 55 mph, has a normal reaction time of ¾ of a second plus a perception time of 0.8 second, and is traveling over a road with a friction coefficient of 0.4, it will take a minimum distance of 378 ft to stop. That stopping distance is 16 ft farther than the driver can see, so he will apply the brakes too late to avoid an accident. If the perception time had exceeded 0.8 second, the driver would overrun his stopping distance by another 81 ft for each added second of perception time. If the driver had been using the high beams on his headlights he could see 428 ft down the road and would have adequate time to stop his vehicle. So, don't be lazy about changing from low beam to high beam whenever the traffic will permit you to do so. Don't drive with the handicap of inadequate vision at night.

Some rather unpleasant things can happen if you don't "buckle up for safety."

7 RESTRAINT SYSTEMS

This chapter has been included not primarily to make you a better driver but in an attempt to keep you a live one. It is not completely true that a restraint system will not make you a better driver, because it *can* during an emergency or loss-of-control maneuver. During a spin-out or broadside slide you can be thrown from the steering wheel by the deceleration forces caused by the skidding, broadsiding tires. If you cannot steer, you will not have a chance to recover control of the vehicle. With a lap belt, or pelvic restraint as it is known in automotive circles, your body will remain in place behind the wheel, but you will have to restrain the upper part of your body by holding onto the steering wheel. Your feet will probably be thrown violently to one side or the other, but you will be able to retain control of the steering wheel and still have a chance to make a recovery. *If* you don't panic, you will be able to make a recovery and regain control of the vehicle during a violent spin-out or broadside slide. Experienced drivers are knowledgeable about turning into their skid or broadside slide, but you can't do it if you don't have your hands on the steering wheel because you are "plastered" against the right hand door.

Most people resent being forced to wear restraint systems. They don't wear them because they feel that the accident is going to happen to the other guy. "I'm too good and smart as a driver for it to happen to me!" If you believe that and act that way, then you are kidding yourself and playing a very dangerous game. There may be that one vehicle that is going to spinout into your lane on rain slick roads or some other unavoidable, no-fault accident that can seriously injure or kill you. To avoid death or costly and painful surgery to repair crash injuries, always wear your restraint system when you are driving.

Seat belts and other restraint systems are designed basically to prevent or reduce body injury in a severe crash. They do this by grabbing you and forcing you to "ride down" with the vehicle and experience approximately the same deceleration. Despite the protests of the outspoken critics of Detroit, the U.S. manufacturers have done an outstanding engineering job in design. One example is that the front of a vehicle will crush evenly and smoothly and bring the vehicle to a stop without lethal, high level deceleration peaks that can occur with improper vehicle design. Figure 7.1 shows the deceleration-time profile for a full size passenger vehicle hitting a solid concrete wall at 30 mph. This is equivalent to hitting the back of a parked car, of equal weight, at 60 mph. The average peak deceleration for a full size passenger vehicle in this type of 30 mph barrier crash is about 23g's. This level of deceleration is survivable by the occupants *if* there is a restraint system *in use* that will enable them to "ride down" with the vehicle; i.e., experience the same deceleration-time profile as the vehicle.

Engineers talk about "g" forces but what are they? Each of us has one "g" acting on us, pulling us toward the center of the earth as a result of the gravitational pull. That one "g" is our weight when we get on a scale. Now, if we have 23g's acting on us horizontally in a crash deceleration, the force acting on us

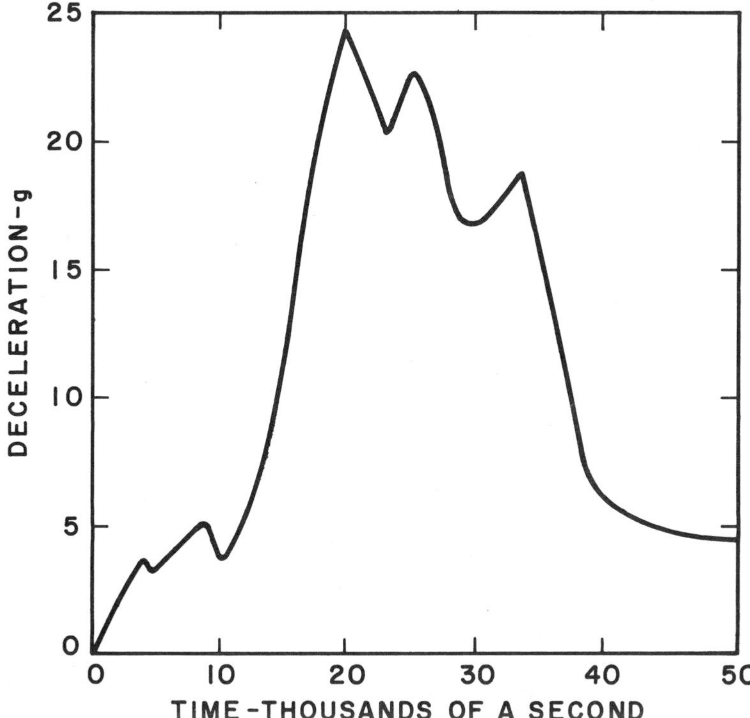

Figure 7.1. This graph is the deceleration-time profile for a standard sedan hitting a solid wall at 30 mph.

horizontally is 23 times our weight. If you weigh 200 lbs the deceleration force is 23 x 200 = 4600 lbs. This force must be applied to your body by the restraint system and the bracing of your arms and legs to prevent you from slamming into the steering wheel, windshield, or instrument panel.

Figure 7.2 illustrates the average crash deceleration force for an average full-size passenger vehicle in a concrete barrier crash at various impact speeds. Somewhere between 30 and 40g's is approximately the limiting deceleration force for occupant survival with a full restraint system. There are wide differences between human beings; their weight in relation to

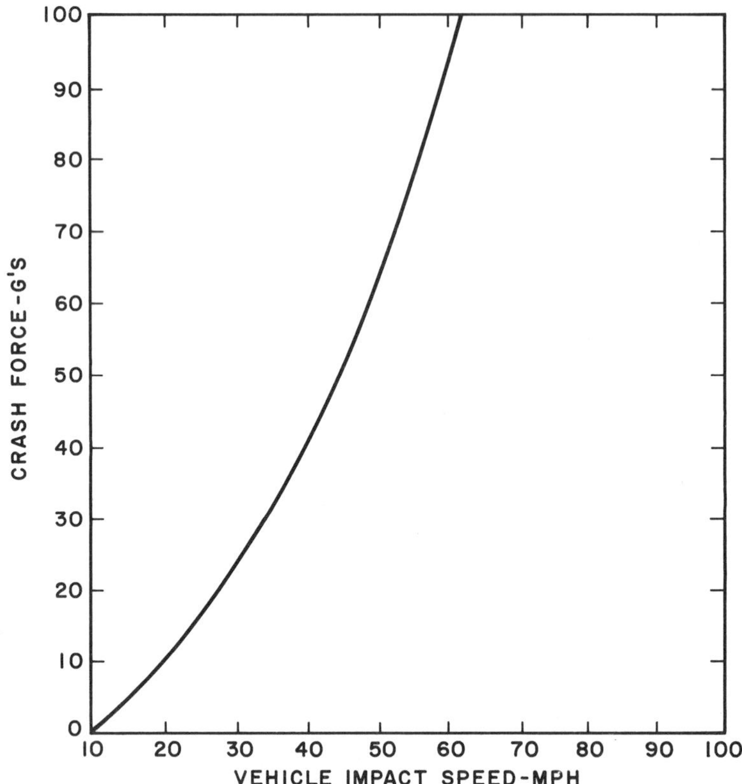

Figure 7.2. Shown here are the average peak deceleration forces for a standard passenger vehicle in a concrete barrier crash at various speeds.

bone structure, strength of bone structure, ability to brace themselves with hands and feet, and condition and strength of the internal organs. One person may survive a crash that would kill others so it is impossible to say that at a certain speed you will live and above that you will die. Unrestrained you probably will not survive a 30 mph barrier crash or you will be seriously injured if you do survive.

It is one thing for this book to say, "Be a good boy and wear your restraint system" and another one entirely for you to know exactly what unpleasant things can happen to you if you are unrestrained during a crash.

Figure 7.3 illustrates an unrestrained driver flying forward during a crash and slamming into the steering wheel and steering column. Although the steering columns in today's cars are crushable under impact, the steering wheel and column can still inflict lethal damage to the occupant. Note the x-ray schematic in the lower right hand corner of the illustration. This shows the large blood filled balloon, which is the heart, slamming against the back of the rib cage. Although the human body is a wonderfully designed piece of equipment the human heart is not particularly well supported within the body cavity. The Creator didn't design us to be slammed into steering wheels and steering columns. For one thing, the heart is heavy when filled with blood and the walls are constantly pumping in and out so there can't be any attachment points to the side walls of the heart. Figure 7.4 shows the type of damage that can occur to the heart when it slams against the

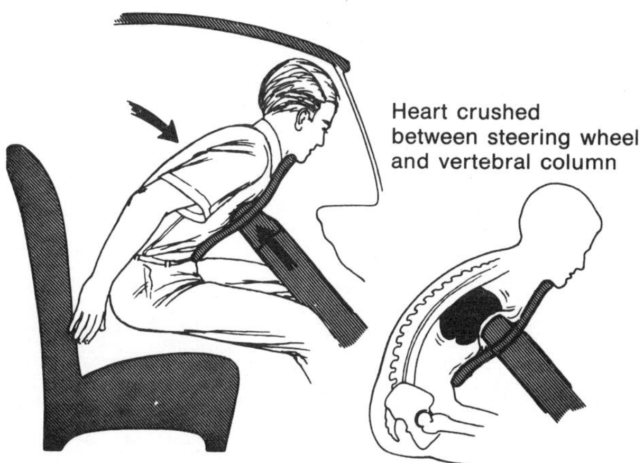

Figure 7.3. This drawing shows how an unrestrained driver slams into the steering wheel and steering column during a crash. (Used with permission of the Society of Automotive Engineers, Inc., Warrendale, Pa.)

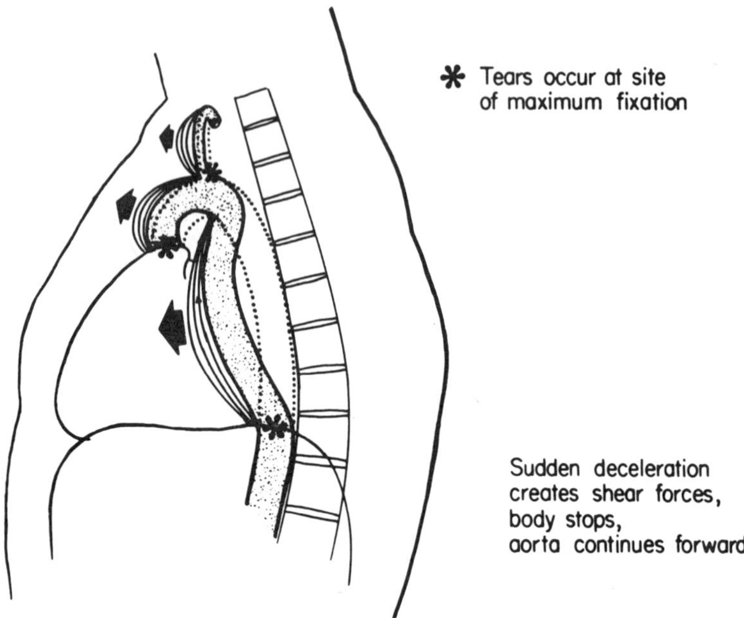

Figure 7.4. Typical cardiovascular damage caused by high deceleration force in a crash. (Used with permission of the Society of Automotive Engineers, Inc., Warrendale, Pa.)

rib cage under high deceleration forces. The heart can literally explode under impact with a resultant rip in the side wall. Death is almost instantaneous. The aorta, the large, blood filled vessel leading from the heart, can tear at a number of places as it slams forward. Tears in the aorta can result in death in seconds, minutes, or hours depending upon the size and location of the tear. Surgical repair of the tear must be performed before the accident victim bleeds to death internally.

Figure 7.5 illustrates the type of rib damage that can occur. The illustration shows the ribs fractured only on one side, but in head-on crashes at high speeds with unrestrained occupants the ribs on both sides can be broken. This is called a "flailed"

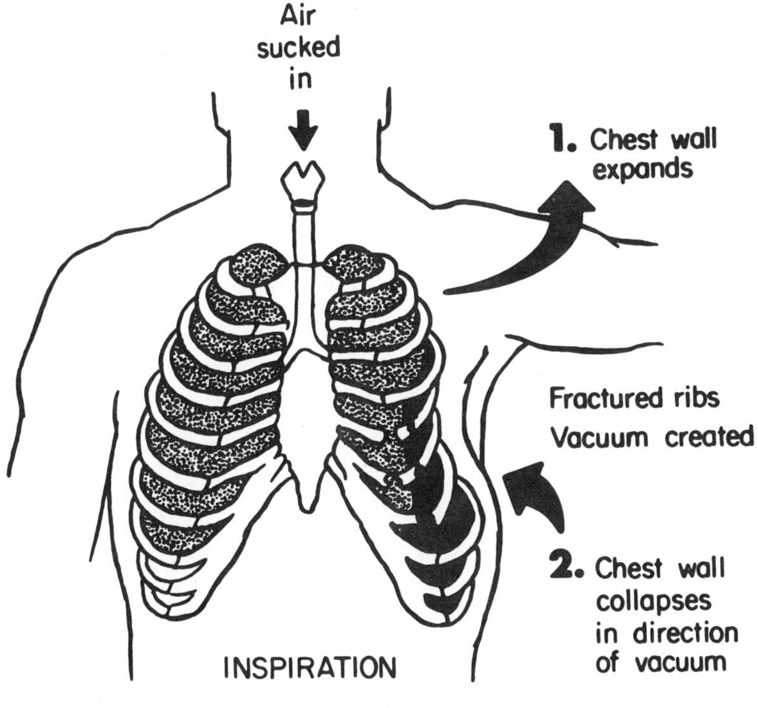

Figure 7.5. Typical rib cage damage to an unrestrained occupant in a high-speed crash. (Used with permission of the Society of Automotive Engineers, Inc., Warrendale, Pa.)

chest and the victim is normally unable to breathe. The sharp ends of the broken ribs may pierce the lungs, which, because of the bleeding, may cause the accident victim to drown in his own blood. The illustration shows collapsing of the lung caused by air being pumped into the chest cavity through a hole in the skin made by a broken rib. The air pumps in during breathing and collapses the lung by building up between the rib cage and the outer surface of the lung. If this happens on both sides the victim dies from suffocation.

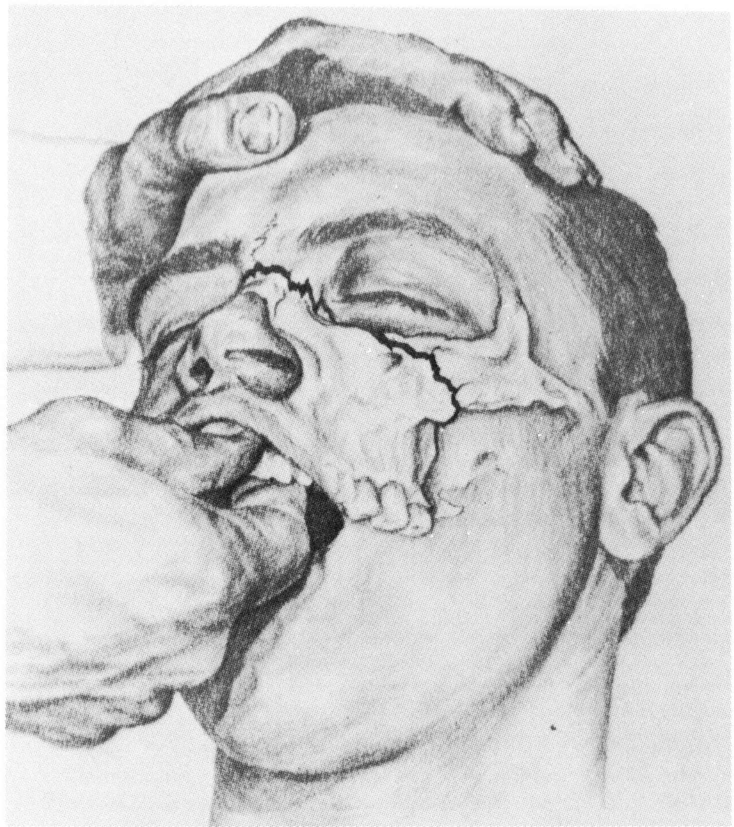

Figure 7.6. Because the skull is not particularly strong in the front, the damage to an unrestrained occupant in a high-speed crash can be extensive. (Used with permission of the Society of Automotive Engineers, Inc., Warrendale, Pa.)

Figure 7.6 shows the damage that can result to the front of the skull when an accident victim slams into the vehicle structure ahead of him under a crash impact. The skull is not particularly strong in this damaged area due to the holes for the eyes, nostrils, and mouth. Figure 7.7 shows the type of surgical repair necessary to put the pieces back together. As one sur-

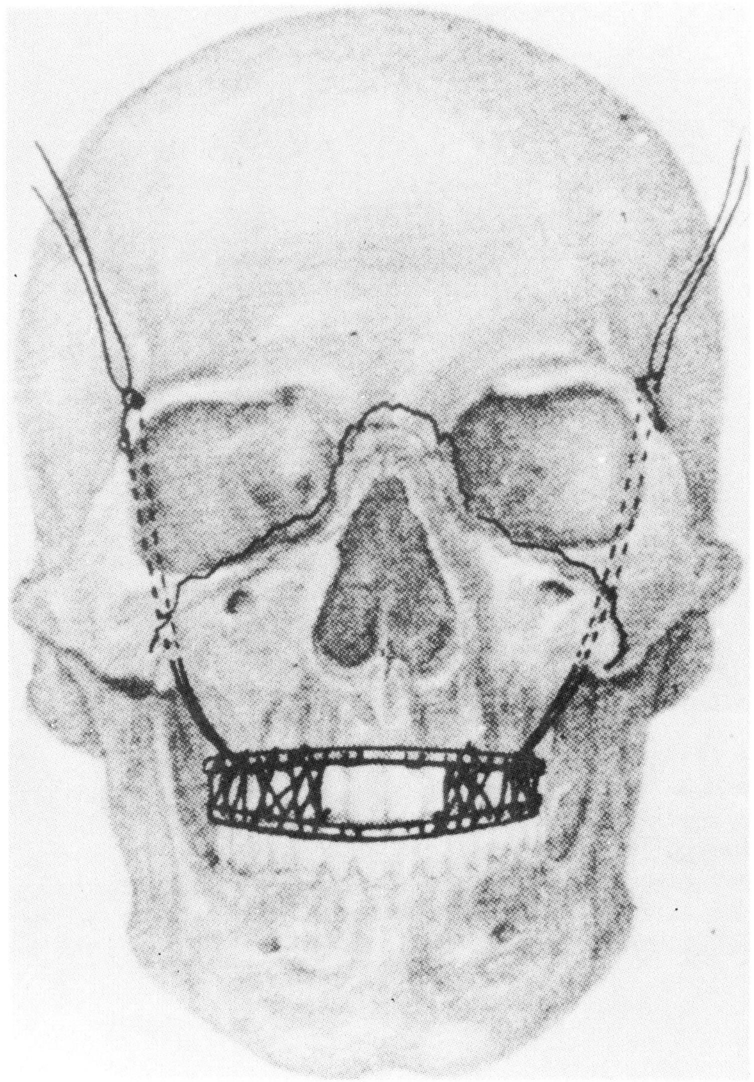

Figure 7.7. The surgery required to repair skull damage often includes wiring the pieces back together.

geon described the operation, "It's like gluing together a tea cup that has been dropped on the floor." The wires through the skull must be left in place for weeks and the time to heal the fractures depends upon the age of the victim. Four to six weeks is normal. While the teeth are wired together the victim must be fed baby food pumped through a tube inserted behind the teeth.

None of these injuries are very pleasant, are they? There are other types of painful and deadly injuries that you can experience, but this book only describes a few of the common injuries experienced by unrestrained vehicle occupants. All of these injuries can probably be avoided by wearing a full restraint system. If you are tempted not to use your restraint system think of the pain, the expense, and the boring hours you could spend in a hospital because you didn't wear it.

The choice is yours to make, but knowledgeable highway safety researchers who know what can happen to an unrestrained occupant in a crash will not even drive around the block without using the available restraint system.

The key is to let the other fellow make the mistake at 120 mph.

8 HIGH SPEED PURSUIT

This chapter discusses points relative to the safe operation of your emergency vehicle in high speed pursuit driving. Your police department probably has a specific policy or training aids dealing with the pursuit and apprehension of suspects and/or traffic violators. It is not the intent of this chapter to supersede your normal operating procedures in this area or to provide a "how-to-do-it" police manual. If the suggestions in this chapter can make you a better and safer driver at pursuit speeds, then it has accomplished its purpose.

Entering into high speed pursuit driving the law enforcement officer will find that this type of driving requires the utmost in skill and understanding of vehicle handling, as well as knowledge of the handling characteristics of the particular make of vehicle he is driving. Driving at speeds of 100-145 mph is not something for the novice law enforcement officer. If he has never driven at these high speeds before and enters into a chase to apprehend a suspect, he is endangering not only his life but possibly the lives of some innocent family. High speed driving, to be as safe as possible, requires practice. If the law enforcement officer has not been trained in high speed driving on a test track when he was receiving his police training, then he should practice on lonely stretches of road to learn "the feel" of a vehicle at high speeds. The vehicle should be driven at progressively higher speeds each practice session in 5 mph increments until the top speed of the vehicle is reached. *Don't* move on up to high speeds immediately. You aren't the reincarnation of Jim Clark even if you think you are. Play it safe and stay alive!

At extremely high speeds the tires are touching only the tops of the humps in the road. Note in Figure 2.17 that the coefficient of friction between the tire and the road surface drops off with speed. This is understandable because the road surface is not "plate glass" level and smooth. It cannot be paved absolutely smooth and the pressure of the tires from heavy traffic pushes parts of the surface down further than others, causing the irregularities in the road. Old roads that need retopping are a perfect example of this. If the tire is only touching the road part of the time, obviously the coefficient of friction will be dramatically reduced at high speeds. Unfortunately, there is little, if any, engineering data on coefficient of friction at high speeds due to the speed limitations on highway tire testing equipment.

At high speeds *don't* brake heavily and attempt to change the direction of your vehicle at the same time. If the wheels lock up in a skid at high speeds you will probably find your vehicle in an uncontrollable broadside slide. There is a case on record in the Department of Transportation accident investigation files where a law enforcement officer did this at approximately 120 mph. He broadsided and spun out for over 700 ft taking down barricades, posts, signs, etc. before rolling down an embankment. Fortunately, he had on his full restraint system and didn't hit anything solid so he walked away from the wreck but his vehicle was a total loss. If there had been a utility pole, tree, or other obstacle in his path he would have been killed instantly. At these speeds, a non-breakaway pole, pipe, tree, or any other solid relatively thin object will slice a vehicle in half like a meat cleaver.

If your patrol area contains curving sections of interstate highway or expressways then you should find the safe limiting speeds through these sections in the early morning hours when the roads are essentially deserted. If the suspect enters into the curve too fast, you will be able to slow your speed so that you can safely avoid his spinning vehicle when he loses control. Don't forget to establish the safe cornering speeds for typical exit ramps. Figures 2.9 through 2.13 illustrate quite clearly the narrow "limit-of-adhesion" speed range through exit ramps of different radii. Use the "comfortable" speed through the corner because you can't gain but a fraction of a second or a second on a suspect by cornering at the absolute limit of adhesion. Let *him* make the mistake and turn his vehicle over, not you!

Unique Effects of High-Speed Driving

Tunnel Vision

One point about high speed driving that is unknown to the average driver is the narrowing of the visual field as the vehicle speed is increased. This occurs because the eye does not form an instantaneous picture. It takes a fraction of a second for the image to develop on the retina so that you can see it. Try moving your hand slowly across in front of your face. You can see it clearly when it is moved slowly. Move it faster and faster back and forth. It does not have to move particularly fast across your visual field before it becomes an indistinguishable blur. You can check the side vision effect by holding your arm out at full length straight ahead of your shoulder. Have the palm down and at a level with your eye. Now move the hand back past the head in about one second. Notice you are unable to see the back of your hand when it is about 30° off center of your visual field. Double the speed of the hand in moving back and it disappears almost as soon as you move it. So it is with high speed driving. At 120 mph plus you are going to be able to see only a few degrees to right or left of your visual field because objects in the side field are moving too fast to register on the retina of your eye. Remember that you are looking down a tunnel at high speeds!

Adrenalin Kick

There is a physical effect of high speeds that is not experienced by the average driver. It is the result of an excessive flow of adrenalin into the blood stream as a result of the excitement and danger of the high speed pursuit driving and apprehension of the suspect. In a long duration pursuit the "adrenalin kick" has two separate effects that can result in possible dangerous operation of an emergency vehicle. First, there is an expansion of the time-speed sense, just as in the case of marijuana intoxication. Every event is slowed down in the driver's evaluation of what is occurring. When he slows down to 90 mph after traveling 140 mph he feels as though the vehicle is only moving at 45-50 mph. If the pursued vehicle spins out, it appears to be spinning in slow motion. The emergency driver is likely to misjudge his safe stopping distance under these circumstances. Second, there is a tendency for the driver to become overconfident in his driving ability and his vehicle when he is under the influence of the adrenalin. The driver is prone to "dash in where angels fear to tread" and to take reckless chances that he would normally avoid. Veteran police officers have experienced the "adrenalin kick" after each exciting pursuit that is sometimes followed by a "shoot-out." The aftereffect is extreme nervousness and difficulty in doing simple things like lighting a cigarette or operating the chamber release to unload their shotgun. So, realize what the "adrenalin kick" is doing to your judgement. Watch your speedometer so that you aren't fooled into thinking you have slowed down to a safe speed.

High-Speed Blowouts

The principal mechanical danger in a prolonged high speed pursuit is the strength of your tires at high speed. Prolonged speeds over 85 to 100 mph require Police Special tires or tires warranted by the manufacturer to retain their strength and integrity at the top speed of your vehicle. The list of tires to check includes radial ply tires because not all radials are made to the highest performance level. The city purchasing agent should obtain a letter from the manufacturer providing a warranty on the tires for high speed driving. If your city is cutting costs by putting straight production run tires on downtown patrol vehicles, *do not* be led into a prolonged high speed chase by a fleeing felony suspect or traffic violator. At 100 mph the average production tires may "blow" in three minutes or less. Figures 4.7 and 4.8 show the reason for this. At high speeds the tires have "standing waves" produced in the treads and the sidewalls at speeds of 100 mph and above. As explained previously, this is as though the tread is being run through a set of rollers at 100 mph or faster. Unless the tire is designed for this punishment, the tread can separate from the cord and the entire tire disintegrate from internal heat due to the "ripple." When one tire "blows" the remainder of them are probably borderline and ready to fail also. A four tire blowout above 100 mph will probably be good for a trip to your friendly mortician. If you have standard production tires on your vehicle, pass the chase on to one of the interstate or expressway patrol cars that are equipped with high speed tires. Stressing your tires at high speed would be a stupid gamble with your life and the lives of other motorists on the road. If you are an expressway patrol driver, and there are mixed tires (Police Special and straight production tires) stored at the police garage, check your tires at the start of the shift to be certain that a mechanic hasn't installed a production tire or two on your vehicle. Mechanics make mistakes also and it could be embarrassing to find it out at 100 mph plus.

In the event of a blowout at high speeds—*don't apply the brakes!* If you touch the brakes you will probably lose control. Let the vehicle roll out to a stop. The vehicle will pull to one side but you can control it. Don't worry about saving the tire because it is already worthless. Just save yourself and your vehicle. After the vehicle coasts down to 20 to 25 mph, pull over off onto the shoulder and brake gently to a stop.

Anticipation and Finesse

At 140 mph your vehicle is traveling 205 ft/sec, or a mile every 25 seconds. Your vehicle is closing with the oncoming car in the opposing lane at 285 ft/sec if it is traveling at 55 mph. When the oncoming vehicle is a mile away your vehicle will pass by the oncoming vehicle in 18½ seconds. What all of this means is that at top pursuit speeds you are traveling up to 2½ times as fast as the maximum federal speed limit of 55 mph. You are *closing fast* on the road ahead. This demands your maximum concentration in attempting to predict the position of cars in the road ahead when you are to get there 18 to 25 seconds later. Under the best possible braking conditions with a dry road it will take a third of a mile or more to stop your vehicle. If trouble is developing a mile down the road you have about 16 seconds, including perception and reaction time, to start braking if you are to stop before you reach the scene. If you are looking only a third of a mile down the road, you may be one second or more late in starting to apply your brakes, so you will be involved in an accident if there is no escape route for you to take. You have to drive with your attention about one-half to one full mile down the road to avoid accidents.

When driving at high speeds, a delicate touch is required in steering and braking. Jam on the brakes or make a quick steering correction at that speed and you will probably throw your vehicle out of control. Start your braking easily and push on the brake pedal progressively harder if the vehicle still remains under full control. If you are driving a vehicle with front wheel disc brakes you have an excellent chance of retaining full steering control almost independently of the rate of brake application. But don't be overconfident and trust them too much. If there is time always start braking easily, gradually increasing your rate of brake application and the total force on the brake pedal. Don't take a chance on starting a spinout at 100 mph plus!

If there are several patrol cars in a high speed pursuit chase—*don't bunch up.* If something happens to cause panic braking, all chase cars could be disabled and the suspect can continue on, laughing to himself. Don't use more than two patrol cars following the suspect at close range.

Another factor to consider, Why are you trying to apprehend the suspect or violator? Is it worth risking your life and the lives of others? The pursuing officers have a soul searching decision to make because they are involved in a game that can lead to violent death and destruction.

Remember that not all of us are born high speed emergency drivers. We aren't all A.J. Foyts who can remain cool, calm, and collected at ultra high speeds. If you are getting extremely nervous, your hands are shaking and your right foot is patting the accelerator pedal, your left foot weighs a ton, and your hands are slipping on the steering wheel from nervous perspiration, face it, *You have reached your limit!* There is only one thing to do, slow down to normal highway speeds or pull over and stop. Things will work out better another day and time. Don't push yourself to operate at high speeds if you are afraid. No one will criticize you for slowing down. It is the *only* intelligent thing to do under the circumstances because you are a hazard to yourself and all other drivers and passengers on the road. You aren't being a coward by acting in the best interests of the driving public.

A brief vehicle inspection
every day can prevent costly,
or even fatal, accidents.

9 MAINTENANCE

Except in a limited scope operation the emergency vehicle driver is not expected to perform routine maintenance tasks and checks on his vehicle. However, the emergency vehicle driver who is planning on a long and happy life uses some of his spare time between runs to inspect his vehicle for indications of unsafe conditions. He knows his life can depend upon the safe mechanical operation of his emergency vehicle. If the driver is on ready-alert, in his uniform, obviously he cannot crawl under the vehicle to check out the undercarriage and suspension components, but there are important inspection procedures that can be conducted without becoming covered with grease and dirt. It is suggested that the following checklist be used at the beginning of your shift. Don't delay a run to complete the checklist, but don't delay following the checklist to discuss everything that happened to the vehicle during your time off.

The checklist should include the following:

1. Tire Inflation Pressures—This is one of the most important checks that you will make. Carry your personal tire inflation pressure gauge because it is very unlikely that one left with the vehicle will stay with it. As explained in the text previously, the vehicle will be uncon-

trollable in a turn with low inflation pressures in one or more tires. It is particularly dangerous in the outer front tire during a high speed cornering maneuver. Balance the front and rear pressures to what you have used before and know will cause the vehicle to handle properly. Slight pressure differences will not be serious but 5-10 lbs can be. Don't forget to check your spare tire.

2. Condition of Tires—Check the sidewalls for blisters, bulges, cuts, broken cords, cracks, or other evidence of reduced tire integrity or strength. Check the tread rubber for any signs of separation from the carcass, cracks in the grooves between ribs, or foreign material imbedded in the tire. Remember that those four small tire footprints control the vehicle. Divide the tire into quadrants, by marking the sidewall with chalk, and have someone drive the vehicle forward. As each successive tread area is exposed, inspect it closely. This is important, don't neglect it.
3. Wheels and Rims—Look for bent rims or wheels. The last driver may have gone over a curb at high speed. A bent rim from hitting a curb probably means dangerous cutting of the cords in the sidewalls that could result in a high speed blowout. Such damage may not be apparent on the tire.
4. Steering Linkage and Wheel Lugs—Put your hands on the front and back of each front wheel. See if you can pivot the wheel back and forth. Loose steering linkage parts can be detected in this manner. With an 8000-lb ambulance you may not be able to turn the wheels. Next put both hands on top of each front tire and try to push and pull it back and forth. "Sloppy" ball joints or loose wheel lugs can be detected in this manner. Do not jack the vehicle up for this check since that will make the ball joints appear "sloppy." Many vehicles have lost a wheel at high speed because a mechanic put the nuts

on finger tight and didn't tighten them down. Put your hands on top of the rear wheels and push and pull them back and forth to check the rear wheel lugs. These inspection procedures can be carried out while checking the condition of the tires. Make a standard procedure of it. Do it the same way each time so you won't forget anything. Ask your supervisor to furnish some check sheets that can be filled out after coming on duty.

5. Under the Vehicle—Check under the vehicle for something out of place or dangling down. This can be done without crawling under the vehicle.
6. Belt Tension—Check the alternator, water pump, cooling fan, and power steering drive belts. Normally, when the belt has the proper tension you cannot push or pull it back and forth more than ½ inch when grabbing it in the middle between pulleys.
7. Radiator Hoses—Move them back and forth and check for signs of cracking or leaking of coolant. Try to move the hose clamps to see if they are tight. If you can reach it, squeeze the middle of the lower hose to see if it collapses. If it does, the suction of the water pump will cause the hose to collapse at driving speeds and the engine will overheat. Normally, there should be a spiral wire inside the hose to keep it from collapsing. If the hose can be collapsed by hand, it should be replaced.
8. Coolant Level—If there is an overflow surge tank, check its level and refill it with the correct coolant if necessary. If there is no surge tank, do the same with the radiator. Note proper levels for both hot and cold; do not overfill.
9. Oil Level—If the oil level is down a quart, add oil. If the oil appears dirty and "sludgy" get the oil and oil filter changed. Again, do not overfill.
10. Spark Plug Leads—See that all leads are seated firmly on the spark plugs.

11. Air Filter—Be certain it isn't clogged with dirt and insects. By bumping it flatly on a concrete floor, you can jar most of the debris loose. Replace if condition warrants.
12. Check the hydraulic fluid level in the brake system reservoir.
13. Check the oil level in the power steering pump reservoir.
14. Battery—Check the electrolyte level in each cell. Add distilled water or water from a water softener if the level is down; don't overfill. Fill only to the bottom of the ring on the filler neck. Occasionally remove the battery leads and clean if corrosion is present. Dirty contacts on the battery leads can give you a "dead" battery when you need an instant start.
15. Wipers and Windshield Washer—It can be dangerous as well as embarrassing to be unable to see because of a sudden covering of the windshield by rain, splattered muddy water, or the impact of a swarm of insects.
16. Front Surface of Radiator or Air Conditioning Condenser Cooling Fins—Butterflies, moths, grasshoppers, and other insects can block off your cooling air and cause overheating and aborting of your emergency run. Pick them off or blow them off with high pressure air or water. A wire brush is handy for removing deeply imbedded insect carcasses from the cooling fins.

Take care of your vehicle and it will take care of you. Remember, when you are on an emergency run you need all the help you can get!

INDEX

A

Adhesion, 59
- limit of, 1
- relative, radial & cross-bias ply tires, 60

Alcohol, 81
- blood-alcohol nomograph, 99, 101
- driver intoxication level, 97
- safety action program, 81

Apex of turn, 33

B

Belt tension, 124
Belted-bias ply tire, 57
Blood-alcohol, 97-101
Blowouts, high-speed, 119
Body
- crash damage, 109
- position, of the driver, 92

Brake
- disc, 41
- drum, 39
- fade, 38
- "locking up", 47
- "pumping," 53

Braking
- anti-skid devices, 53
- effect on cornering force, 21
- for an unexpected turn, 52
- left foot, 95
- panic, 15, 39, 47

"Breakaway"
- borderline, 60
- sign supports, 83
- speed in a curve, 27

Build-up in front of
- non-rotating tire, 85

C

Cardiovascular damage
- in a crash, 110

Center of gravity
- of vehicle, 13, 71

Centrifugal force, 13
Closed loop systems
- driver-vehicle, 4
- environment-driver-vehicle, 5

Coefficient
- effect of rain, 44
- of friction, 29, 30, 42

Code 3 run, 33
Conduction of heat 39

Cornering
at high speeds, 26
force on a tire, 10
force of various designs, 61
speeds for various
turn radii, 28
techniques, 23
vehicle in a turn, 12
Crash deceleration
force in "g's", 107
Crash injuries
cardiovascular damage, 110
rib cage damage, 111
skull damage, 112
Cross-bias ply tire, 56

D

Deceleration limits
for human survival, 107
Deceleration-time profile, 107
Diminishing radius
exit ramp turn, 37
"Dirt track", 21
Distance
minimum following, 48
stopping, equation, 42
Drift angle
tire, 10
vehicle, 15
Driver position, 92
Driving traction, 20
Drugs
effects of on
driving performance, 102
prescription, 100

E

Effects of high-speed driving, 117
Energy
heat, 39
kinetic, 39
Escape route, 82, 89
Exit ramps
constant radius turns, 35
diminishing radius turns, 37

F

Fatigue, 103
Feet, position of, 95
Following distance, 48
Footprint area of the tires, 7
Force
centrifugal, 13
cornering, 10
"g", 106
side, 110
Friction
coefficient of, 29, 30, 42
Fuel saving, 62

G

"g" forces, 106
"Groove," locked into the, 33, 34

H

Hand position
of driver, 93
High-speed driving, 115
High-speed cornering, 26
Hydroplaning
minimum speed, 77
tire, 74, 76

I

Ice, glare, 43

Injuries, crash
cardiovascular, 110
rib cage, 111
skull, 112
Intoxication
recovery time, 97, 98

K

Kinetic energy, 39

L

Lag, steering, 11
Lap belt, 105
Law of momentum, 85
Leaving the road, 82, 89
Limit of adhesion
cornering, 1, 22-28
cornering speeds for various turn radii, 28

M

Maintenance, 122
Marijuana, 103
Modular design ambulances, 72
weight advantage in crash, 88
Momentum, law of, 85
Murphy's Law, 81

N

Neutral steer, 70
how to determine, 73
Night vision, 104

O

Oversteer, 70
how to determine, 73

P

Panic braking, 15
Pelvic restraint, 105
Perception time, 104
Physical condition, 96
Pneumatic trail of tire footprint, 18
Prescription drugs, 100
Psychotic drivers, 79
Pursuit driving, 115

R

Radial ply tire, 56, 57
Radiation, heat, 39, 40
Radius
constant, 35
diminishing, 37
Reaction time, 47
Reflections in store windows, 80
Restraint systems, 105
Rib cage damage in a crash, 111
"Ride down," with the vehicle, 106
Rolling contact, 7
Rolling resistance, 62

S

Side force on a tire, 10
Skull damage in a crash, 112
Speed
its effect on cornering, 26
"breakaway," 27
Spin-out, 60, 72
Standing wave of tire, 64
Steering
angle, 15
lag, 11

recovery, 35
response with radials, 61
Stopping distance
equation, 42

T

"Tailgating," 48
Time-Speed Sense
distortion of by marijuana, 103
distortion of by adrenalin, 118
Time,
perception, 104
reaction, 47
Tire
belted-bias, 56
blow-out at high speeds, 119
cornering force, 10
cornering force vs inflation pressure, 68
cross-bias ply, 56
deflection, 63
design, 55
drift angle, 10
effects of non-rotating, 85
footprint area, 7
footprint distortion, 17
free rolling, 20
how it steers, 9
hydroplaning, 74
increased mileage, 62
inflation pressure, 66, 122
pneumatic trail, 18
police special, 65
radial ply, 56
ripple, 63
roll-under in a cornering, 67, 69
side force, 10
"squirming," 57
standing wave, 64
Traction, driving, 20
"Tuning" tire with inflation pressure, 73, 74
Tunnel vision, 117
Turn, apex of, 33

U

Understeer, 70
how to determine, 73

V

Vehicle
center of gravity, 13
cornering, 12
crush, 106
drift angle, 15
Velocity change, 85-87
Vision, 104

W

Weight, advantage in crash, 88